Mr. Robot:
A Binge Guide to
Season 1

*An Unofficial Viewer's
Guide to USA Network's Award-Winning
Television Show*

by *Greg Enslen*

Copyright © 2019, V.190606PB

\

Mr. Robot: A Binge Guide to Season 1

Introduction

We are living through a great time for television. Right now, there are almost too many good shows on television to watch all of them. Over the last few years, with the growth of more outlets and cable networks, you would think there would be fewer good shows, a limited supply of them, spread out over more networks. Instead, it seems like there's been some sort of renaissance in television, with new and unexpected shows coming from every direction.

One of the stand-out shows of late is USA Network's **Mr. Robot**, a show that started off quietly and quickly built a following with its trippy visuals and convoluted plot lines. Word spread quickly and the show became an underground sensation, growing in popularity and going on to win the **2016 Golden Globe** for **Best Television Drama**. Leads Rami Malek and Christian Slater were both nominated for Globes, with Slater winning. The show was also nominated for the Emmy Awards.

The show centers around hacker Elliot Alderson and his involvement with an underground hacker collective known as "fsociety." The group is hellbent on taking down the multinational conglomerate E Corp., the largest company in the world. As Elliot is drawn deeper into the plot, he encounters strange characters that seem to know more about him than would seem possible.

The show itself can be a roller coaster, and I found it challenging to remember all the callbacks and subtle hints and clues the show's writers used to foreshadow upcoming plot twists. Those callbacks and background details led me to write this book, another in my **Binge Guide** series. Like **Game of Thrones** and another USA Network's show, **Suits**, **Mr. Robot** benefits from multiple viewings. With the help of this guide, you'll be up to speed in no time. Well, I'm off to change all the passwords on my computer—if watching **Mr. Robot** doesn't make you paranoid about computer security, nothing will.Unless noted, all filming locations are in New York City.

-

How to Use This Binge Guide

This binge guide will walk you through **Season 1** of USA Network's hit show **Mr. Robot**.

I designed this book to replicate the experience of watching the show with a knowledgeable friend—one who has already seen the show and interjects occasional pieces of information and trivia, but studiously avoids ANY spoilers or hints about what's to come.

To Get Started:

☐ Buy this book.

☐ Queue up the first episode of season 1

☐ Open the book to the first episode—but don't read ahead! "There be spoilers here."

☐ Start watching. I've broken up the episode narrative into sections.

☐ As you watch, refer to the relevant section.

☐ After each section, I have added any **relevant information on casting and characters, interesting quotes, goofs made during production, filming locations and any other notes** pertaining to that particular scene or series of scenes.

☐ In some cases, all of the scenes set at the same location are grouped under one header. If you start to read about something you haven't seen, STOP and go back to watching the show.

☐ Continue watching until the show is over.

☐ At the end of each episode, I offer my **critique** of the episode, along with more notes on the episode in general and links to more information.

One of the strengths of Mr. Robot is that it keeps you guessing. You can never be *quite* sure you trust what you're watching or what you're being told. Elliot is not the most trustworthy narrator. That makes the show a delicious and offbeat take on normal television narratives. In fact, the audience is practically another character on Mr. Robot—don't be surprised with Elliot starts talking directly to you. The show is apt to throw something crazy at you with little or no warning—and for those who haven't seen the episodes multiple times, you might miss the meaning of a particular character or phrase.

Dive in, root for your favorite character, and enjoy!

One more thing: For consistent naming of season

and episode numbers, I use the Internet's standard numbering system for television show episodes, but it can be a little confusing. You'll see numbers that look like "S01E02" - in this case "S01" stands for Season One and "E02" stands for Episode 2, so **S01E02** means the second episode of season one. I'll use them for cross references and the like, so keep an eye out for those episode identifiers, usually in bold. In addition, Mr. Robot has **very strange episode number and titles** written in computer code—if you get lost, check this ebook's table of contents.

Thanks, and if you enjoy this Guide, let me know. I'd love to hear from people who find this book interesting or helpful. I can be reached at **greg@gregenslen.com** or via my website at **gregenslen.com**. You can also send me feedback or report any typos or missing/contradictory information at the website.

Enjoy!
- Greg Enslen

Episode One – "Hello Friend"

Episode Number: S01E01

Original Air Date: June 24, 2015 (released on-line May 27, 2015)

Time: 64 minutes

Synopsis: By day, Elliot works for a cybersecurity firm, but in his downtime, he uses his hacking skills to bring justice to the wicked. He's approached by a mysterious underground group—they want his help to bring down a massive international conglomeration he's been paid to protect.

Opening Scene

The show begins with a blank screen and a voice. **Elliot Alderson**, a down-on-his-luck cybersecurity engineer, is imagining us, the audience, into existence.

He warns that "you're only in my head," then adds that "we have to remember that." With the opening lines, the audience realizes that this person is mentally troubled and has a somewhat tenuous grasp on reality.

Elliot goes on to tell us he's passing along to us "top secret information" on a group of men who are "secretly running the world," speaking over a montage of scenes of corporate bigwigs arguing in a conference room.

We see Elliot for the first time on a subway on his way to work. Adorned in a dark hoodie, he's convinced two men on the subway are following him. He thinks about a mistake he made—last night he was supposed to go to a friend's birthday party, but he went elsewhere.

Notes: The group of men shown as "controlling the world" are not random—it is a group of directors and lawyers Elliot will soon encounter. The first face the audience sees in the entire series that of Tyrell Wellick.

Characters: Elliot is played by **Rami Malek**, best known for playing **Ankmenrah**, an ancient Egyptian Pharaoh in the **Night at the Museum** series of movies. He got his start with roles on **Gilmore Girls** and season eight of **24** and also appeared in films such as **Short Term 12**.

Quotes: Elliot: "What I'm about to tell you is top secret. There's a powerful group of people out there that are secretly running the world. I'm talking about the guys, no one knows about the guys who are invisible. The top 1% of the top 1%. The guys that play God without permission. And now I think they're following me."

Ron's Coffee

Elliot is waiting in a coffee shop when **Ron** walks in

and sits down. Others recognize him—Ron's the owner of this and a chain of similar coffee shops. Elliot moves to his table and sits, telling Ron he likes his coffee shop.

He also tells Ron that he's hacked Ron's entire computer network, mentioning this as if it's not a big deal. Elliot's learned that Ron is a major peddler of child pornography. Elliot explains that he knows what it's like to be different, but that doesn't excuse what Ron is doing. Elliot explains his father died of leukemia caused by the company he worked for, although Elliot couldn't prove it.

Ron thinks Elliot is blackmailing him. He offers to pay, but Elliot stands, telling Ron he isn't in it for the money—in fact, he's already called the police, who show up just as Elliot leaves.

Walking home, Elliot considers himself a good hacker who uses his preternatural skill with computers to right the wrongs of the world.

Notes: Ron started Ron's Coffee shops six years ago, but his name is Rohit Mehta. Now he has 17 shops with eight more opening in the next quarter. Interestingly, when Elliot is talking about the coffee shop's stellar Internet access speeds, he uses the past tense—"I like coming here because your wi-fi was fast"—perhaps indicating that he won't be coming to Ron's shops any more or assumes they're about to go out of business. In fact, the wi-fi was so fast Elliot got curious why a coffee shop would need a connection that fast, leading him to hack Ron's networks and discover a website Ron operated called "Plato's Boys." Elliot copied everything on Ron's network—all the emails, files and his cache of 100 terabytes of child pornography he serves to his 400,000 users—and tipped off the police.

Filming Locations: The scenes at "Ron's Coffee" were filmed inside a real coffee shop—**Think Coffee**, located at 123 4th Avenue in New York City's East Village.

Quotes: Elliot: "That's where you're wrong, Ron. I don't give a shit about money." **Elliot:** "It's good. So good, it scratched that part of my mind. The part that doesn't allow good to exist without a condition."

Terminology: Tor is free software for enabling anonymous communication. The name is derived from an acronym for the original software project name "The Onion Router." **Onion routing protocol** or "Onion routing" is implemented by encryption in the application layer of a communication protocol stack, nested like the layers of an onion. Tor encrypts the data, including the destination IP address, multiple times and sends it through a virtual circuit comprising successive, randomly selected Tor relays. A **Sysadmin**, or system administrator, is a person who is responsible for the upkeep, configuration, and reliable operation of computer systems, especially multi-user computers, such as servers. **Afk** means Away from Keyboard, Internet slang for doing something away from the keyboard and out in the real world.

Subway to Work

We're back on the subway with Elliot, who is convinced he's being followed by two men who keep glancing at him. Elliot thinks the "higher ups" don't want someone with his "powers" running around. Suddenly a homeless guy starts talking to Elliot, calling him "kiddo" and telling him that we live in "exciting times." Elliot ignores him.

Later, Elliot walks into work at **AllSafe Cybersecurity**, telling us that he only hacks at night. By day, he's a "regular cyber security engineer." He passes through a cubicle farm of other workers, including the employee sitting next to him, **Lloyd**. Elliot's called into the office of **Gideon Goddard**, the manager. Gideon is talking to **Angela Moss**, another employee and a friend of Elliot's from childhood. They are arguing over another hack of **E Corp**, which occurred overnight, and what they should do about it. Someone is attacking the E Corp. servers on a weekly basis. Gideon is unsure whether or not Angela can "handle" them as a client and chastises Elliot about him not following the office dress code.

Angela is mad at Elliot—he stood her up the night

before and didn't come to her birthday party at a local bar. He's painfully antisocial and we see, through a flashback, that he went to the bar but was too self-conscious to go inside.

She says "stop thinking about something else" and he says he's thinking about work. She says Gideon likes him—he thanks Angela "all the time" for bringing Elliot in as an employee—but also says she thinks Elliot secretly hates working there. In his head he agrees—he likes most of the people but hates that he works to protect corporations. He lies and says "I love it here" and she knows he's lying and they both laugh.

Angela's also concerned about herself—she says she's late on her last two student loan payments and can't get Gideon to give her a raise. Her boyfriend **Ollie Parker** joins them—Elliot hates him and excuses himself. Ollie tells Angela that he knows Elliot hates him and thinks Elliot is in love with Angela.

Notes: The show's creator, **Sam Esmail,** can be seen in the subway scene—he's wearing glasses and standing to the right of Christian Slater's character. Elliot is AllSafe employee #ER28-0652. On most TV shows, when a character has internal dialog, the other characters are oblivious. In this scene, Angela calls him out for "thinking about something else" and waits impatiently for his voiceover/internal thoughts to finish. It's almost as if she can hear him thinking and is waiting for him to be done.

Characters: The homeless man is played by **Christian Slater**, best known for appearing in such films as **Interview with a Vampire**, **Heathers**, and **True Romance**. Angela Moss is played by **Portia Doubleday**. Gideon Goddard is played by **Michel Gill**, who also appeared in **House of Card**s as President Walker. Ollie Parker is played by **Ben Rappaport**.

Filming Locations: On the street, Elliot passes the **Pig 'n Whistle Irish Pub** on 3rd Street in New York City. It opened in 1969. There actually many restaurants and pubs with very similar names—another is located at 202 West 36th Street. There was also a famous Pig 'n Whistle located in Hollywood that closed in 2011. From inside the offices of AllSafe, you can see the facade of the **Mobil Building** at 150 East 42nd Street. According to **Untapped Cities**, the building was the former headquarters of the oil company.

Quotes: Ollie: "I can't have that kind of negativity in my life."

Terminology: A **Rudy Attack** uses a particular Denial of Service tool to execute massive numbers of slow attacks to bring down network— RUDY stands for "R-U-Dead-Yet" and is named after an album by Finish melodic death metal band **Children of Bodum**.

"We Are Cowards"

Elliot meets with his court-appointed psychiatrist and therapist, **Dr. Krista Gordon**. She talks about the first time he came to see her. Elliot isn't listening—he's thinking about how easy it was to hack her and gain access to all of her accounts. Elliot thinks that she's bad at reading people even though she's a psychologist; she is recently divorced and apparently has horrible taste in men. She's been "dating losers on Eharmony," and her latest is **Michael Hanson**. Curiously, Elliot could find nothing about him on-line, "no LinkedIn, no Facebook," and something about Hanson bugs Elliot.

Krista says that Elliot's not "yelling like before," which is good, and tries to get him to talk about his feelings, but he's reluctant to share. She says he has lots of anger issues, including being mad at society. Elliot thinks "F*ck Society," and Krista says he has a lot to be angry about, hinting at a troubled past.

He likes Krista, telling her she understands what it's like to be alone. Elliot realizes he's said too much, saying things he shouldn't know about her. They discuss him going to the party last night, and Elliot lies, saying he enjoyed himself and even got a girl's phone number. She says he's "hiding again" and warns him that when he's hiding, "the delusions come back." She also asks about his sightings of "the **men in black**," and he lies, saying the meds she's given him are working.

Notes: It is unclear if Dr. Gordon is a psychiatrist or psychologist, but she is acting as his **court-appointed therapist** and can prescribe medication. Krista's password is Dylan_2791, her favorite singer and her birth year backwards. Her Eharmony account describes her as a "buxom" single woman, aged 44, who is looking for men 39-50 in New York City. She's Hispanic and Catholic, doesn't smoke, drinks socially, and doesn't want kids but its "OK if my partner has kids." During Elliot's tirade against our modern society, it appears that he's talking to Krista and finally opening up, but we learn he's just imagining telling her what he really thinks. And he starts off his speech by saying "I don't know," but it's clear he has plenty to say. When he talks about how "all our heroes are counterfeit," we see videos of **Lance Armstrong** (accused of doping in 2012), **Bill Cosby** (accused by upwards of 60 women of rape or sexual assault), and **Tom Brady** (suspended by the NFL over 2015's Deflategate).

Characters: Krista is played by **Gloria Ruben**, an actress and talented singer. According to IMDB, she toured with Tina Turner as a backup signer and sang the Canadian national anthem at the 1998 baseball All-Star game.

Quotes: Krista: "What is it about society that disappoints you so much?" **Elliot:** "Oh, i don't know. Is it that we collectively thought Steve Jobs was a great man, when when we knew he made billions off the backs of children? Or maybe it's that it feels like all our heroes are counterfeit. The world itself is just a big hoax. Spamming with our running commentary of bullshit masquerading as insight, our social media faking as intimacy. Or is it that we voted for this? Not with our rigged elections, but with our things, our property, our money. I'm not saying anything new. We all know why we do this, not because Hunger Games books make us happy but because we wanna be sedated. Because it's painful not to pretend, because we're cowards. F*ck society."

Terminology: Eharmony is a popular on-line dating website used by Krista. The **Men in Black** are a mythical group of government agents dressed in black suits who perform clandestine activities—they were also the subject of a popular film series.

Meeting E Corp

Back at AllSafe, Elliot is working when he's approached by Angela's boyfriend, Ollie, who is making an effort to befriend Elliot and asks him to lunch. Elliot passes, and Ollie wants things between them to be less awkward. Elliot doesn't mind if things are awkward—he's not a fan of Ollie's for several reasons: Ollie likes George W. Bush, **Transformers 2: Revenge of the Fallen**, the music of

Josh Groban and Maroon 5, and the movie **The Hangover**.

Ollie's also cheating on Angela with a woman named "Stella B." Elliot has thought about telling Angela but decides against it: she has "shitty taste in men" and Elliot's not quite ready to see who she dates next. A group of people arrive from **E Corp**, the largest conglomerate in the world, to discuss the latest hack of their servers. E Corp, which Elliot refers to as "Evil Corp," has contracted with AllSafe to handle cybersecurity. Gideon shows **Terry Colby**, the Evil Corp CTO and **Tyrell Wellick**, among others, around the office ahead of their meeting. Tyrell, the Evil Corp Senior Vice President, Technology, chats with Elliot—and Elliot's impressed: Tyrell is an actual techie, using a Linux system and knowing his way around a computer.

Notes: Ollie's password was "the easiest to hack" as it is "123456Seven." In discussing E Corp and their reach, Elliot sees computer monitors, tablets, cell phones and laptops manufactured by the company. In his mind, E Corp is "Evil Corp" and from this point forward, the show follows that conceit, changing all future logos and mentions of the company, even by other people, to "Evil Corp." The logo for E Corp, a capital letter "E" turned askew, is nearly identical to the corporate symbols for Enron, an American energy company that went bankrupt in 2001. The "E" is also very similar to the "e" in "Dell," another computer company. Elliot is one of six on-site engineers on the E Corp account. As for Elliot's internal dialogs, Wellick doesn't wait patiently for them to be over; he actually interrupts one in this scene and correctly guesses what Elliot is thinking.

Characters: Tyler Colby is played by **Bruce Altman**, best known for appearing in such films as **Glengarry Glen Ross** and **Matchstick Men**. Tyrell Wellick is played by Swedish actor **Martin Wallstrom**.

Quotes: Wellick: "So I see you're running Gnome. You know, I'm actually on KDE myself. I know this desktop environment is supposed to be better, but you know what they say: old habits, they die hard. It's going to be fun working with you."

Goofs: Elliot doesn't think much of Terry Colby because he still uses a Blackberry, although these devices are favored by many for their secure communications.

Terminology: Gchat is short for Google Chat, an instant messaging service which was renamed Google Talk and then replaced with Google Hangouts. A **Blackberry** is a mobile phone and messaging device and was the first widely-available device with keyboard—it was so popular for a while, it was known as a "crackberry." **Linux** is a Unix-based open source operating system and the primary alternative to Microsoft's Windows and Apple's Mac OS. **KDE** and **Gnome** are two of the more popular desktop environment applications of Linux which allow the user to create a Windows-like desktop interface for manipulating the files and programs on their computer.

Shayla

After work, Elliot heads home and thinks about "saving the world." His version of that is freeing everyone from their financial shackles and all of their personal debt. Inside his dingy apartment, he feeds his fish **Qwerty**. Later, when he's crying uncontrollably, he wonders what normal people do with their sadness and loneliness. He assumes normal people reach out to friends and family, but that's not an option for him. We see a flashback of him and his mother— she's smoking and holding his arms down and doesn't seem very loving. Instead, Elliot does **morphine**, and goes on to explain how he can use it without getting addicted.

He realizes he's out of **Suboxone** and calls **Shayla**, his neighbor and dealer, who comes over and delivers more. She says it's "on the house" but Elliot pays her, not wanting to be in her debt. She mentions she tried to find him on **Facebook** but he says he doesn't have an account. She offers him some Molly and they end up sleeping together. After, Elliot says that you shouldn't ever "make decisions when you're on morphine."

Notes: Outside Elliot's apartment, there are two signs

on the building next door that read "Prime Commercial Space Available - E Realty Corp," showing again just how large—and insidious—E Corp is. To keep from becoming a Morphine junkie, Elliot limits himself to only 30mg a day. He also checks every pill for purity and has 8mg of Suboxone "for maintenance" in case he goes through withdrawals. In my research, I was unable to find out exactly how that works, but several websites talked about doctors prescribing Suboxone to treat withdrawal from opiates such as morphine. Unclear on the show, it may mean that Elliot is taking them together, or alternating between the morphine and the Suboxone to prevent addiction. The **Promises Treatment Center** has a lengthly page on Suboxone Maintenance and how their detox program works: they use Suboxone alone for 7-14 days with patients interested in breaking their opiate addiction without suffering acute withdrawal symptoms.

Characters: Elliot's mother is played by **Vaishnavi Sharma**. Young Elliot is played by **Jack Corbin**. Shayla is played by **Frankie Shaw**.

Filming Location: According to **Untapped Cities**, Elliot's apartment is located at 217 E. Broadway on the Lower East Side. In the background, you can easily spot the distinctive One World Trade Center tower.

Quotes: Elliot: "Sometimes I dream of saving the world. Saving everyone from the invisible hand, the one that brands us with an employee badge, the one the forces us to work for them, the one that controls us every day without us knowing it. But I can't stop it. I'm not that special. I'm just anonymous. I'm just alone."

Terminology: Morphine is an addictive opiate. **Suboxone** is a prescription drug used often to help with withdrawal symptoms or as a less-addictive alternative. **Molly** is the street name for the psychoactive drug MDMA, more commonly known as **ecstasy**.

A Dinner Date

Laying next to a naked Shayla, Elliot gets an alert on his phone: Krista, his psychiatrist, is out on a date with **Michael Hanson**. Elliot dresses and leaves, going to the restaurant. While observing Krista and Hanson, Elliot also spots two "men in black" watching him from a nearby cafe. Hanson and Krista exit the restaurant and Hanson hails a cab. Elliot, pretending to be Hanson, calls the cab company and gets Hanson's home address. The homeless man appears again and accost the "**men in black**," begging for spare change. At Hanson's address, Elliot runs into Hanson mistreating his little dog and asks to use his phone, saying he needs to call his mother. Instead, he uses the encounter to get Hanson's phone number by calling his own number and seeing it come up on the screen. He deletes his outgoing call and hands the phone back, thanking him.

Notes: Michael Hanson's cab number is 56Y2 and his home address is 306 Hawthorne. Hanson's phone looks to be running an altered variation of iOS: the icons are similar and have similar coloration, although the "Phone" app shows a camera aperture icon and the "Storage" icon looks a lot like the icon for Dropbox. The time on his phone reads 2:12AM. There is also a "B of E" app, which implies a Bank of E Corp. According to the phone, Elliot's phone number is (212) 555-0179. Hanson's phone call history include calls to people named Jacob Medary, Bernadette Pino, Adam Brustein and Drew Wood.

Characters: Michel Hansen is played by **Armand Schultz**.

Filming Location: Krista has dinner with Michael Hanson upstairs at **Pierre Loti**, a real wine and tapas bar located at 300 East 52nd Street in Midtown East. Pierre Loti operates two other locations in New York City. The two "men in black" observe Elliot from the outdoor seating at the nearby **Gulluoglu Baklava and Cafe**, located at the corner of Second Avenue and 52nd Street.

Goofs: When Elliot is looking at Hanson's phone before making the call, the display only shows the time and cell signal strength. After the call, when he's deleting the number, it shows the sound level (muted) and the battery level.

Another Hack

On is way home from Hanson's house, Elliot gets a call from Angela—another hack of E Corp has begun. This time it's a DDOS attack. She and Lloyd are at the office, trying to stem the damage, but she needs Elliot's help. Arriving later, Elliot gets up to speed. Lloyd says it's the "worst DDOS attack" he's ever seen.

Gideon arrives and wants to know what's going on and where the attack is coming from. "Everywhere," Elliot answers. "USA, Finland, Thailand, Kuwait," then goes on to say that it's a new kind of attack: a rootkit. It's a set of instructions installed inside the company servers that can "delete system files and stop programs." It also can replicate itself like a virus. Gideon realizes they need to fly to a server farm near Washington DC to stop the attack. He takes a private jet and takes Elliot with him.

Notes: Judging by the shape of the home button, Angela is using an iPhone. She's calculated that for every hour the Evil Corp servers are down, the conglomerate loses **$13 million**. And, by the way, we actually see the Angela character use her mouth to say the words "Evil Corp," so we are clearly seeing whatever Elliot is seeing and hearing, even though in "real life" she probably said "E Corp." Angela reads an article on-line about the "massive" corporate hack of Evil Corp, which includes trending information from **Google+** and **Daily Beast**. Gideon tells Angela to "call Prolexic" for help, presumably another cybersecurity firm.

Goofs: It is unlikely, given her IT background and position at AllSafe, that Angela would not be familiar with a rootkit or what it is capable of.

Terminology: A **DDOS attack** is a distributed denial-of-service attack, using multiple computers to flood a single server's bandwidth or resources to shut it down. The **DNS** is the Domain Name System, the decentralized naming system for websites and other locations connected to the Internet. **"Stopping the services"** means shutting down all the **underlying programs running inside an operating systems**, such as error detection, file system manipulation, program executions, and communications.

Server Farm

At Dulles Airport in Washington, D.C., Gideon and Elliot arrive at the Evil Corp server farm. Elliot assists them in shutting down every server and then rebooting them in the proper sequence.

While investigating the network, Elliot discovers a small computer file embedded in the system from an organization calling itself "fsociety." Thinking it's a joke—the name is close to what Elliot said in the psychologist's office—he opens the file. It's the culprit behind all the recent hacks—and he finds a cryptic message to leave the file in place on the server. Not sure if he should delete it or not, Elliot decides to leave it but makes it so that he is the only person who can access the file remotely.

Later, on the flight home, Gideon thanks Elliot and opens up to him, telling Elliot that he's gay. Elliot isn't sure what, if anything, to say.

Notes: Evil Corp represents 80% of AllSafe's business—if they lose Evil Corp as a client, AllSafe will go out of business.

Terminology: The **root directory** is the primary or top-most directory in a computer file structure hierarchy and the first one accessed by a computer during its boot-up sequence. A **server farm** is a collection of computer servers, usually housed in a protected and climate-controlled facility.

Coney Island

Elliot takes the subway home. He's thinking about how to track down "fsociety" when he sees the homeless man again. He's wearing a jacket with a patch on it that reads "**Mr. Robot**." The homeless man asks if Elliot's had a rough night, and says he's getting off at the next stop. He says Elliot should follow him, but only if he "didn't delete it," talking about the file in the Evil Corp server farm. "If you deleted it, we got nothing to talk about." Curious, Elliot follows.

While waiting on the next train, Elliot wants to know what's going on and if the homeless man, known as Mr. Robot by the patch on his jacket, has been following him. Elliot follows him to Coney Island and an abandoned arcade with the sign "f society" out front. Inside, Elliot and Mr. Robot are greeted by a group of hackers using the arcade as a real-world base of operations. They only hack out of this location and never communicate electronically.

Notes: In the hallway leading to the subway, we see several posters for E Corp, including one that says "We Change the World." Another E Corp sign actually says the words "Evil Corp," so we are starting to see things as Elliot sees them. Next to one of the Evil Corp posters is another poster for a movie called "Villains" with a tag line that reads "Evil Always Wins."

Filming Location: The MTA station is the **Church Avenue Station**. Coney Island, Wonder Wheel,and the "f society" building are all real-world locations at **Coney Island** in southern Brooklyn. The address for the **Fun Society Arcade**, a real location, is the **Eldorado Bumper Cars and Arcade**, 3027 West 12th Street at Coney Island in Brooklyn. It's a real, operating arcade and open to the public. You can even see the blue side door that Elliot enters. The

"Fun Society" sign was added by the producers of the show. All of the interior scenes from the TV show were shot on a set at the Silvercup Studios, located in Queens, New York.

Quotes: Mr. Robot: "My dad was a... petty thief. Never could hold down a job, so, he just robbed. Convenience stores, shops, small-time stuff. One time, he sat me down, he told me something I never forgot. He said, "Everyone steals. That's how it works. You think people out there are getting exactly what they deserve? No. They're getting paid over or under, but someone in the chain always gets bamboozled. I steal, Son, but I don't get caught. That's my contract with society. Now if you can *catch* me stealing, then I'll go to jail, but if you can't, then I've earned the money." I respected that, man. I thought that shit was cool as a little kid. A few years after that, they finally caught him. Sent him to jail. Dies five years later. My respect goes with him. I thought he was free doing what he did, but he wasn't. He was in prison. Just like you are now, Elliot. But I'm gonna break you out."

Goofs: Mr. Robot tells Elliot they're going to Brooklyn when they change trains. Actually, once they're at the Church Avenue station, they're already in Brooklyn. And as the approach the "f society" building, they appear to be coming from the south, in the direction of the ocean. In reality, they would be approaching it from the **Coney Island/Stillwell Avenue Station**, located two blocks north. They would travel south from the Stillwell Station on Stillwell Avenue, cross Surf, and then make a left on Bowery to reach the fsociety arcade location.

 Terminology: A **dat file** is a small data file containing computer information in a text or binary format. **IRC** is Internet Chat Relay, and IRC contacts would be people that Elliot knows through the various channels and communications hubs that use IRC to communicate. **IRL** is "in real life," meaning out in the real world. **O-Megz** is the name of a fictional hacker group similar to **LulzSec**, an infamous group of hackers that was brought down when one of the founders, an hacker known as **Sabu**, was arrested and turned in other members of LulzSec as part of a plea deal. **VPN sessions** would be a reference to using a **Virtual Private Network** to anonymize communications over the Internet.

Movie Night

 Later, on the way home, Elliot thinks he's crazy. "That didn't just happen, right?" He's worried and scared and says that he's saying "all this to an imaginary person," meaning the audience. He finds Angela on the steps to his apartment. She wants to watch his favorite movie—**Back to the Future 2**—and smoke some weed. He invites her in and they find Shayla still there—she was at his apartment when he left to spy on

Krista and Michael Hanson's date and she's still there, sleeping. Angela says it's "good" he's dating someone and leaves, telling Elliot to "have fun."

Elliot asks Shayla to leave and begins researching "Mr. Robot" and fsociety and their location—but he can't find much. The building ownership is murky, owned by a company called "Fun Society Amusement, LLC" for 13 years before the owner was shot and killed eighteen months ago. He prepares a envelope of incriminating evidence similar to the one he created on Ron, planning to turn in fsociety.

Notes: Elliot's favorite movie is Back to the Future 2. Angela says she misses Qwerty, Elliot's fish. The fsociety building is located at "3027 West 12th Street, Coney Island" and Elliot's Google search shows the map and correct location, although the actual Google address for the search is obfuscated with dummy text in the address bar. Elliot's bookmark bar in his browser includes links to the BBC, Huffington Post, NY Times, Google News, 4chan and reddit. The article about the shooting death of the "Fun Society Amusement" arcade mentions that he was shot in the back three times and the estimated time of death was 3AM. The article quotes a local resident, Bernadette Pino, with saying "I took my kids there all the time. He was warm and friendly." There was also a Bernadette Pino listed in the recent call history on Michel Hanson's phone when Elliot borrowed his phone. The article also mentions that the name of the owner wasn't released to the press—and in the last lines of the article misspells the word "neighborhood" as "nieghborhood."

Goofs: The Back to the Future 2 DVD box cover is not the actual artwork from the DVD box and there is no "Special 2015 Silver Edition" of the film.

Terminology: 4chan is an anonymous on-line photo sharing website. **Reddit** in an on-line discussion website. An IP or **Internet Protocol address** is the unique numerical label assigned to each device connected to the Internet—including Terry Colby's IP address would allow researchers to trace the hack back to a particular computer.

Wonder Wheel

The next day, he returns to fsociety and is greeted by Darlene, another hacker. He asks her where to find her boss, **Mr. Robot**, and she tells him to "cut the bullshit" and wants to know when he'll give them access to the root directory. She says she wrote the rootkit Elliot found on the Evil Corp server and still needs to "put Colby's IP in the dat file." They plan to make it look like **Evil Corp CTO Terry Colby** is behind the hack.

Mr. Robot arrives and takes Elliot on a ride on the **Wonder Wheel**, a main attraction at Coney Island. While aloft, they have a lengthy discussion about fsociety's plans.

Elliot says he's planning to turn them in, but Mr. Robot doesn't think so—he thinks Elliot feels trapped by money and by corporations. He says fsociety is going to do something about it: they want to wipe Evil Corp's servers. Evil Corp owns 70% of the global consumer credit industry. Done correctly, it would erase every financial record of "every credit card, loan and mortgage" held by them. Paper records would be out of date and unenforceable; with that, every citizen would be instantly debt free, the largest single transfer of wealth in the history of the world.

Elliot realizes fsociety needs his help. Mr. Robot tells him that tomorrow, AllSafe is going to get a visit from the FBI and U.S. Cyber Command. Mr. Robot wants Elliot to change the dat file he found to make it look like Terry Colby was behind the hack.

Returning home, Elliot's in a great mood. He passes the Evil Corp posters in the subway again, including one where a student is worried about how she's going to repay her student loan. At home, he checks Angela's bank accounts with E Corp—he apparently has access to them as well— and finds she owes them nearly $200,000 in student loans. He creates two envelopes of information—one incriminates fsociety, while the other incriminates Terry Colby and would set into motion the fsociety plan.

Notes: Mr. Robot says he scored "the last bag of

Twinkies from Gristedes." This might be a reference to the temporary disappearance of Twinkies from store shelves in 2012, although the dates don't really match up. According to Wikipedia, Twinkie production was halted by Hostess Brands in November 2012 during the company's bankruptcy proceedings. They became available again in July 2013 and production resumed.   Gristedes is a New York City-based chain of small supermarkets that began operation in 1891. Angela Moss attended the fictional Brooklyn Institute of Technology.

Characters: Darlene is played by **Carly Chaikin**.

Filming Location: Elliot and Mr. Robot go for a ride on the famous **Deno's Wonder Wheel** located in Coney Island. While they're on the ride, you can see several wide shots of the area around Coney Island and the nearby Luna Park, including the beach, the **Coney Island Cyclone** and Thunderbolt roller coasters. You can also see other rides that surround the real-world Deno's Wonder Wheel, including the Spook-A-Rama and Bumper Cars.

Goofs: While perusing Angela's Facebook page, it says that Elliot and Angela are "friends" and that they have 40 mutual friends. This implies that he in fact does have a Facebook account, but he told Shayla he didn't have an account. It's possible he is accessing Facebook through someone else's account, but they would have to be "friends" with Angela and have many friends in common with her. The date on the on-line newspaper shows 22 January 2015, and mentions in the sidebar a "military jet crashes in Lincolnshire." An American F-15 did crash in Lincolnshire, England, but the crash occurred in October of 2014, so it's doubtful it would be in listed in the "top stories" sidebar three months later. Terry Colby's terminal IP address is **218.108.149.373**, but there are too many digits in the last number—they typically only go up to 256, so this is a fake IP address.

Terminology: The **U.S. Cyber Command**, part of the United States armed forces, centralizes military command of cyberspace operations and synchronizes digital defense of U.S. military networks.

Incrimination

On the way to work the next morning, Elliot sees more "men in black" and the poster for the movie "Villains" again. At AllSafe, they meet with the FBI, U.S. Cyber Command, and people from Evil Corp, including Terry Colby and Tyrell Wellick.

Elliot is planning to turn in fsociety and places the envelope with the incriminating evidence on the table in front of him. Angela begins explaining the hack and AllSafe's response to it but is cut off by Colby and unceremoniously booted from the meeting. Elliot defends her but Colby says she's "not going to work out for us, not at this level." Angered, Elliot switches envelopes—Wellick notices this as well—and passes the information that will incriminate Colby to the FBI.

Notes: AllSafe first noticed the breach at 2:07AM. Lloyd began working on the hack from the AllSafe offices at 2:35.

Terminology: The phrase "**terminaled in**" means to access the servers remotely from a terminal.

Hansen

Nineteen days later, Elliot is angry—there have been no arrests in the hacking case, even though he gave the FBI enough information to lead to Terry Colby. Everything is the same as it was. He visits **fsociety** but finds no Mr. Robot and no other members of the hacking collective. He continues hacking Michael Hanson and realizes it's not his real name. Elliot confronts "Michael Hanson," exposing his lies and infidelities. Elliot tells him to break things off with Krista—or he'll send digital proof to his wife and the police. One of the women he dated was underage—Elliot made up that part, but it was close enough to the truth for Hanson to believe it. And Elliot has one more request: **the dog, Flipper**.

Elliot copies all of his Michael Hansen files to a DVD and puts in his "digital cemetery," a DVD storage binder, the kind with pages that hold eight DVDs each. There are lots of

DVDs in the storage binder, each full of files on someone he's hacked in the past. Each is labeled with a different label, the name of an actual musical group and album.

Notes: Krista Gordon heads her own company, Gordon and Associates. Michael Hanson lives in apartment 2C, likes the Yankees, and his dog is named **Flipper**. Angela Moss is friends with women named Patricia Cannon and Jennifer Edwards, and her Facebook profile page doesn't show any photos of Elliot. "Michael Hanson" is actually **Lenny Shannon** and he's cheated on his wife with at least seven different women, one of whom was underage. Some of the DVDs in Elliot's "collection" include: The Doors, People are Strange; Boston, Don't Look Back; Tom Petty and the Heartbreakers; Pink Floyd, Wish You Were Here; AC/DC, Back in Black, Fleetwood Mac, Rumors; and Van Halen, among others.

Filming Location: Elliot confronts "Michael Hansen" across the street from Peak Thai. This is a real **Thai restaurant** located at 301 East 49th Street in NYC.

Goofs: When looking at Krista's profile, it says they are "friends" and also have 40 mutual "friends." This repeats the same issues from earlier with Angela's Facebook profile—either Elliot really has a Facebook profile and has 40 mutual friends, or the producers of the TV show used the same fake header to replicate a Facebook-like website. There are misspellings here as well: the profile says she studied IT at the "Institute of Psych and Madness" in NY. This is unlikely as she is billed as a doctor and psychiatrist. It also says she attended "Sheepshead bay high school." It also says that Krista is in a relationship with "Michael Hanson" and the font in blue, indicating that they are friends and that he has a profile on Facebook, but Elliot clearly stated early on that he couldn't find a Facebook account for the man.

Terminology: A **dictionary brute force attack** is a technique to discover a password or other authentication mechanism by guessing thousands or millions of combinations—it's actually called a dictionary attack, and a brute force attack is slightly different. **Ashley Madison** is an on-line dating website for people looking to have affairs; ironically, the actual site was hacked sometime in July 2015, just after this episode aired. Since the hack, Ashley Madison has re-branded itself.

Evil Corp

The next day, Elliot meets with Krista and can tell she's been dumped. At work, Elliot tries to talk to Angela, but she's embarrassed about what happened in the Evil Corp meeting. And she's mad that he stood up for her—it was nice, but it made her feel like she couldn't do it on her own. They hug and everyone in the office is looking at them—until Elliot and Angela realize the people are looking at the TV monitor behind them: Terry Colby has been **arrested** for the hack of Evil Corp. In **Times Square**, Elliot is giddy to see multiple reports on the large screens of Colby's arrest—and doesn't notice the large black SUV that pulls up behind him.He thinks he's being arrested, but the men from the SUV take him to **Evil Corp**, where he's taken to a conference room that overlooks the city. **Tyrell Wellick** is waiting for him there with a group of lawyers. Elliot looks at the camera and pleads to the audience: "please tell me you're seeing this, too."

Notes: The group of men shown in the conference room, Wellick and his lawyers, is the same group of men shown in the out-of-focus opening scene of the episode when Elliot imagines a group of evil men that control the world.

Characters: The CNBC reporter on TV is played by **Gigi Stone**. Mr. Sutherland, the head of the Evil Corp team, is played by **Jeremy Holm**.

Filming Location: Evil Corp is located at the corner of Lexington Avenue and East 57th Street in NYC. The exact address is 135 East 57th Street. According to **Untapped Cities**, this is the same building used as the offices of Norman Osborn in the first **Spider-Man** movie.

-------------------------------------—

Critique:

What a great way to introduce a main character—he dreams us, the audience, into existence, making us a co-conspirator in his future activities. Elliot is lonely and desperate to make a mark on the world, but he's painfully anti-social and seems barely capable of operating in the "real" world. But he's got some things going for him—he's wildly talented in the hacking arts, and possesses a moral compass of sorts that requires him to fight evil and dream of ways to balance the scales of the world.

As the episode progresses, we learn that he's working both sides of the equation. By day he works to protect the computer systems of corporations he despises, including the aptly-named "E Corp," an updated amalgamation of Microsoft, Enron and Goldman Sachs. At night he's a "white hat," bringing down child porn distributors and outing cheating husbands. He's unsure of how to operate in the world and unsure of what to do with all of his loneliness. Rami Malek is a talented actor, imbuing Elliot with a depth of emotion while simultaneously hiding most of his emotions or displaying them only in scenes where he's fantasizing about actually sharing his opinions with the world. The scene with Elliot crying alone in his apartment is a powerful one, rare in modern television—the main character is so raw and emotional, at least in that scene, that we can allow ourselves to excuse his questionable behavior and lack of social graces.

His love for Angela is obvious, and her protectiveness almost torpedoes their relationship when he stands up for her in a high-level meeting. Angela understandably wants to stand on her own two feet, but Elliot isn't good at social situations, so when he leaps into the conversation, it's with two feet and without abandon. His awkwardness is evident only moments earlier, when the CTO of the largest corporation on the planet thanks him for stopping the latest hack, and Elliot's response is an awkward "okay." Not "thank you" or "that's very nice" or even a nod—Elliot seems genuinely confused about how to respond to a compliment.

By the end of the episode, Elliot's on his way to making new friends, starting with the mysterious Mr. Robot. The discussion between him and Elliot on the Wonder Wheel is fascinating, cutting back and forth between them as they discuss the central conceit of the show—how to balance the scales of society through a massive act of wealth redistribution. I have no idea how they filmed that scene—clearly each side of the conversation must have been filmed separately as they rode in the car, but the interaction between them is palpable. I'll chalk it up to insanely good editing and two very good actors.The pieces are coming together, and Elliot's sly switching of envelopes during the meeting with the FBI sets in motion a plan that could result in the largest revolution in the history of the world—or get everyone involved with fsociety imprisoned for life.

Episode Notes:

From the beginning, you'll notice many things that are different from "regular" TV shows. One of them is the naming convention for each episode, each rendered in what I like to call "computer speak."

For example, Episode One is called "Hello Friend" in the credits but elsewhere is referred to what looks like a computer file name: "**eps1.0_hellofriend.mov**." These are intentionally jumbled together and often intersperse numbers for letters and vice versa. For example, in episode three, the title transposes a "3" for what is supposed to be a lower case "e," something often done by computer users and gamers. There are no blank spaces—often in password fields, there are no blank spaces allowed, so here they use an underscore—and end with a particular type of video file suffix. ".mov" is the file identifier for Quicktime movies, etc. For ease of reading, I'll use the "English" translations for episode titles.

The title of the episode refers to computer users— often, the first piece of code or program they write in a new computer language is called a "Hello Friend" or "hello world" program, one that prints out the words on the screen.

According to Yahoo, the pilot aired on June 24th but was available On Demand for almost a month before that date to build awareness of the show.

The producers of the show frequently mention Facebook and show on several occasions a website with a very Facebook-like interface: it replicates the layout and design of a Facebook profile page but there are subtle differences. Elliot also refers to the page as "Facebook" and reads off a list of "Facebook Likes" from Ollie's page as evidence of him being an idiot. With the way the page is laid out, with an "about" and "photos" section on the left, a "friends" and "following" area along the top, the positioning of the profile photo and background, and the chronological list of posts along the right side, it's clear we are meant to presume that this is Facebook.

References:

NOTE: All sites accessed on August 18, 2016.

Deno's Wonder Wheel at Coney Island.
http://www.wonderwheel.com/information.html#verticalTab4

Gulluoglu Baklava and Cafe.
http://www.gulluoglubaklava.com/manhattan/

Hopes and Fears, Mr. Robot: every title and episode, explained.
http://www.hopesandfears.com/hopes/culture/television/216489-mr-robot-episodes-titles-explained

IMDB.

http://www.imdb.com/title/tt4652838/?ref_=ttep_ep1

Mr. Robot Wikia.

http://mrrobot.wikia.com/wiki/Mr._Robot_Wikia

Peak Thai Restaurant.

http://www.peakthairestaurant.com/

Pierre Loti Midtown.

http://midtown.pierrelotiwinebar.com/

Pig 'n Whistle on 3rd.

http://www.pignwhistleon3.com/

Promises Treatment Centers, Suboxone Maintenance and detox methodology.

https://www.promises.com/treatment-programs/suboxone-opiate-detox/

Think Coffee. http://www.thinkcoffee.com/locations

TutorialsPoint page on Operating System Services.

http://www.tutorialspoint.com/operating_system/os_services.htm

Untapped Cities, NYC Film Locations for USA Network's "Mr. Robot."

http://untappedcities.com/2015/07/29/10-nyc-film-locations-for-usa-networks-mr-robot/

Wikipedia, several pages.https://en.wikipedia.org/wiki/Main_Page

Episode Two – "Ones and Zeroes"

Episode Number: S01E02

Original Air Date: July 1, 2015

Time: 47 minutes

Synopsis: After a meeting with Tyrell Wellick, Elliot continues to investigate Evil Corp. fsociety comes up with a plan, while Elliot must deal with Shayla's unstable drug supplier.

A Job Offer

Elliot stands in a conference room at Evil Corp, watching as **Tyrell Wellick** and a group of men take their seats around a circular table. Wellick greets Elliot and says he's interested in making Elliot a job offer as head of cybersecurity for Evil Corp. Elliot is unsure, and Wellick asks the others to leave, then tells Elliot that Wellick has just been named the new Evil Corp interim CTO. He tells Elliot that they're going to be moving to handling all cybersecurity internally, which means they'll be canceling their contracts with outside vendors, including AllSafe. Elliot passes on the offer, and Wellick is visibly upset.

Men from Evil Corp drive Elliot home. Outside his

apartment, Elliot's neighbor and drug dealer **Shayla** is being harassed by her drug supplier, **Fernando Vera**. Inside, Elliot takes some morphine and gets to work hacking Tyrell Wellick. He finds it particularly easy, then realizes it might be a trap. He destroys his computer hard drives and microwave the SIM cards in his phone to destroy any evidence of his hack.

Notes: Tyrell Wellick's password is olofsson66, his wife's maiden name and Sweden's independence date, 6-6. Tyrell Wellick's email address is "**tyrellwellick@evilcorp-intl.com**," and we see it on the screen, so either we're starting to share Elliot's delusions—the "real" email address should end with "ecorp.com" or "e-corp.com"—or we're actually looking through his eyes and his brain is replacing every occurrence of "E Corp" with "Evil Corp" before we get to see it. Wellick's "Facebook" page shows he attended the **KTH Royal Institute of Technology**, is married to Joanna Wellick, and is from Vastra Gotaland Ian, Sweden.

Characters: Fernando Vera is played by **Elliot Villar**.

Filming Location: According to **Untapped Cities**, the board room scene was shot at the Trump Soho, located at 246 Spring Street in New York City. Checking out the hotel website, you can review their **meetings section and see photos of the SoHi conference room**—it's at the top of the building on the 46th floor, measures 34 x 56 feet, and features a 13 foot-high ceiling.

Quotes: Tyrell Wellick: "Give a man a gun and he can rob a bank. Give a man a bank and he can rob the world."

Goofs: When Elliot reviews Wellick's "Facebook" profile, we see the same issues that cropped up in the last episode. It shows that Wellick and Elliot are "Friends" and, in this case, share 1,362 mutual "friends." But it's been expressly stated that Elliot doesn't have a Facebook page, so it's impossible for him to be "Friends" with Wellick or share any "friends" in common. Also, that seems like an inordinate number of shared friends. Technically, Sweden doesn't have an independence day, but they do celebrate "National Day" on June 6th.

AllSafe

At work at AllSafe cybersecurity, Elliot is rewarded with a salary bump by his supervisor, **Gideon Goddard**, for his actions in saving the company. Gideon also asks about the **dat file**, but Elliot says he "didn't know what he had."

fsociety is now a known entity in the world—they've gone public with an anonymous video, threatening to release thousands of documents and corporate secrets unless Evil Corp and the FBI meet their demands: the FBI frees former Evil Corp CTO **Terry Colby**, and Evil Corp must forgive all outstanding debt, dissolve their corporation, and donate all their assets to charity.

Outside the AllSafe offices, an unemployed musician is hocking copies of his "unreleased album," begging passersby to listen to his music. **Angela** and **Ollie** are chatting when they run into Elliot leaving work. Ollie congratulates him and invites him to dinner at Morton's, but Elliot, seeing two "men in black" approaching, hastily agrees. Ollie and Angela are surprised and suggest a double date with Elliot's "friend" **Shayla**. After Elliot leaves, the musician convinces Ollie to take a copy of his CD.

Notes: Elliot's desk was in a different location in the AllSafe offices in the last episode—in fact, the cubicle farm where he works seems to have been completely rearranged or moved to a new location. The voice on the fsociety video is clearly that of Mr. Robot. Ollie only has 48 followers on **Twitter**, but there are "some taste makers in there."

Characters: The street musician Cisco is played by **Michael Drayer**.

Filming Location: The exterior shots of the AllSafe building are from the **Trump SoHo Hotel**, located at 246 Spring Street in New York City. The "1109" marker outside was apparently added for the production—the actual location has an address of 246 and sports a **sculpture** in the same spot.

"What's the Plan?"

At his apartment, Elliot finds **Darlene** taking a shower. Elliot leaves his dog, Flipper, with Shayla. On the subway, Elliot is curious how Darlene knows where he lives, but she seems confused. She also explains that she doesn't live anywhere right now because the person she was dating proposed to her. They get off the subway, then at the last second get back on, leaving two men in black on the platform. Elliot isn't sure if she sees them as well—all Darlene says is that she likes to "stay on her toes."

At fsociety HQ, Elliot's worried about his safety but enters to applause—everyone is thanking him for his awesome work. **Mobley**, **Trenton**, and **Romero** are there, along with **Mr. Robot**. They all want to know what's the next step in the plan, and are curious about **Steel Mountain,** the highly-guarded physical location where they store Evil Corp's tape backup files. Mr. Robot discusses the plan with Elliot—they plan to blow up Comet, a natural gas plant in Albany located next to Steel Mountain.

Elliot is dubious, but Mr. Robot plans to confuse Evil Corp with multiple data dumps of embarrassing inside information. After that, they'll hack the controls of the natural gas plant, causing a pipeline explosion. The "Dark Army" is covering Evil Corp's redundant backups in China. If everything is destroyed at the same time, Evil Corp will be brought down. Elliot refuses to kill anyone and leaves, even though Mr. Robot gives him an ultimatum—help or he's out of fsociety. Elliot leaves, worried that he's too involved, and looks to the audience for help, pleading with us to start looking for solutions.

Notes: On the subway, all the stops are obscured on the posted MTA map. Darlene's having a fight with her boyfriend because he won't let her get a turtle. Mr. Robot reminds Elliot that Evil Corp "slowly killed" his father and that Elliot did nothing about it. And he calls his father a zero.

Characters: Although we've seen them before, this is the first time when Elliot meets and interacts with the other members of fsociety. Mobley is played by **Azhar Khan**, Trenton is played by **Sunita Mani**, and Romero is played by **Ron Cephas Jones**.

Quotes: Mr. Robot: "Are you a one or a zero? That's the question you have to ask yourself. Are you a yes or a no? Are you going to act or not?" **Elliot:** "Yo... you've been staring at a computer screen way too long, homie. Life's not that binary. Isn't it?" **Mr. Robot:** "Sure, there are grays... But when you come right down to it, at its core, beneath every choice, there's either a one or a zero. You either do something or you don't. You walk out that door, you've decided to do nothing, to say no, which means you do not come back. You leave, you are no longer a part of this. You become a zero. If you stay, if you want to change the world, you become a yes. You become a one. So, I'll ask you again: are you a one or a zero?"

Terminology: Steel Mountain is a fictional company—the closest real world analog is probably **Iron Mountain**, a large records management and data backup company that maintains several underground and above ground storage facilities under very tight security. A **K-hole** is a slang term for an extreme state of dissociation from the body after getting high on the drug **ketamine**—it can also produce vivid hallucinations and altered states of consciousness in the user. A **PLC** is a programmable logic controller, a small computer usually used in industrial environment. The **Dark Army** is a fictional group of Chinese hackers who will hack anyone for a price.

Shayla and Fernando

Back at Shayla's apartment, Elliot wants to retrieve his dog but instead is drawn into a long and tense conversation with **Fernando**, Shayla's supplier. Elliot's already hacked him—the man is one of "the worst human beings" Elliot's ever known. By comparing tweets from Fernando and his gang with local crimes, Elliot cracked their simplistic code and learned they were responsible for a wave of robberies and murders. He's thought about turning him in, but Fernando is Shayla's only **Suboxone** supplier.

After Fernando leaves, Elliot finds Shayla asleep in the bathtub. Elliot's worried she was raped, but Shayla doesn't mind—Fernando gives her a good deal on the drugs. Elliot's conflicted about taking out Fernando, but decides it's more important than keeping him around as a source of drugs.

Notes: Fernando's user name is "bigpapi6969" and his password is "eatadick6969." Elliot's browser bookmarks bar now shows saved pages including IRC, toolKit_drk, BBC, HufPo, NYT, whitePaper, and classDefs. Elliot says he could go back to digitally counterfeiting prescriptions, something he clearly used to do, but it's more difficult and less successful.

Goofs: Another "Facebook" page and more problems: again, it shows that Elliot is "friends" with Fernando but Elliot doesn't have a Facebook page.

Two Paintings in the Waiting Area

Elliot chats with his court-appointed psychiatrist, **Dr. Krista Gordon**. She wants him to open up, and he compares his options to the two **paintings** in her waiting room—when both choices are bad, which one do you choose? While talking to her, we learn that he's turned in Fernando and his crew by sending information through an anonymous tip on the NYPD's website. Elliot becomes increasingly agitated as

Krista pushes him to open up, and finally he yells at her. Later, he researches climate control systems.

Quotes: Elliot: "How do we know if we're in control? That we're not just making the best of what comes at us, and that's it? Trying to constantly pick between two shitty options? Like your two paintings in the waiting room. Or...Coke and Pepsi? McDonald's or Burger King? Hyundai or Honda? Hmm. It's all part of the same blur, right? Just out of focus enough. It's the illusion of choice. Half of us can't even pick our own...our cable, gas, electric. The water we drink, our health insurance. Even if we did, would it matter? You know, if our only option is Blue Cross or Blue Shield, what the f*ck is the difference? In fact, aren't they...aren't they the same? No, man...our choices are prepaid for us, long time ago."

Ollie and Angela

At Angela and Ollie's apartment, Angela hangs up the phone. She's been trying to call Elliot but he's not picking up. She's worried about him. Ollie is trying to get the street musician's CD to play, but it keeps freezing up his laptop. He gets an email from his other girlfriend, **Stella B**, and hides the screen from Angela, only half listening as she shares her concerns about Elliot.

Ollie makes an excuse to leave, but he's really going to meet up with Stella. As he leaves, we see the street musician

Cisco watching through the camera on Ollie's laptop—something on the CD has allowed Cisco to **commandeer Ollie's laptop** and hack everything on it, including the camera. He watches Angela climb into the shower. Afterward, he types in Chinese to a contact, saying "we're in."

Notes: This is the first time we see where Angela and Ollie live. Ollie sneaks out to see Stella by saying he's going to see his "Arizona buddy Fred."

Coney Island

Back at the Coney Island boardwalk, Elliot finds Mr. Robot sitting on a railing above the rocky beach, reading from a book. Elliot's found a way to hack Steel Mountain without blowing up the pipeline. Mr. Robot says he walked away and is out of fsociety but wants to know how Elliot's father died. Elliot tells him—his father worked at Evil Corp as a computer engineer. He came down with leukemia but made Elliot promise to not tell anyone, not even Elliot's mom. After Elliot let the secret out, his father pushed him down and broke his arm. Elliot's father never spoke to him again and died several months later.

Mr. Robot empathizes with Elliot's father. "Don't you think you deserved it for betraying his trust?" Elliot starts to say that he was only eight years old when Mr. Robot pushes him off the railing to the rocks below.

Notes: Similar to how his father treated Elliot, Mr. Robot also pushes him and causing serious injuries.

Filming Location: Shot at Coney Island, it's easy to see the **Parachute Jump Tower** in the background of several angles. Built for the 1939 World's Fair, riders paid 40 cents to ride one of the eleven parachutes to the top. The ride closed in 1964 and has been owned by the City of New York ever since.

Goofs: In real life, the Coney Island pavilion where Elliot and Mr. Robot chat doesn't extend over a sharp fall to rocks and the beach below.

-------------------------------------—

Critique:

This second episode picks up moments after the first one ended, and brings with it a quick offer from the enemy: a job offer, that is. Elliot passes and Wellick is clearly troubled with his answer, although if Elliot were truly interested in taking down Evil Corp, wouldn't he jump at the chance to fight from inside the belly of the beast?

Two parallel stories appear on Elliot's radar at the same time—fsociety announces its existence to the world, demanding Evil Corp close down. At the same time, Elliot must deal with Shayla and her unstable drug supplier,

Fernando Vera. I liked this side story but felt it was wrapped too quickly—the evidence Elliot submitted to the NYPD must have been pretty compelling for them to cancel one of their donut runs and arrest Fernando and his crew. That also assumes that no one on the police payroll was on the take or looking the other way on behalf of Fernando's crew.

I'm also unsure of Elliot's quick decision to give up Suboxone—he seems to have thought it all out, and it's the best solution for him at the time. As anti-social as he is, it's a leap to think that he's so worried about Shayla—clearly, she's not that concerned—that he's willing to take on a local drug gang and give up his only tool to control his addiction.

Mr. Robot has a plan to take out the physical location where Evil Corp's backup tapes are being stored, and that sounds like a pretty exciting episode of Mission Impossible to me. Or maybe one of the Arnold Schwarzenegger movies where, as he escapes with the tapes, dangling from a helicopter, the entire Steel Mountain explodes in an orgy of fire.

Episode Notes:

The title of the episode refers to binary code—ones and zeroes—and Mr. Robot's comments on making choices.

References:

NOTE: All sites accessed on August 20, 2016.

IMDB.

http://www.imdb.com/title/tt4686038/?ref_=tt_ep_pr

Mr. Robot Wikia.

http://mrrobot.wikia.com/wiki/Mr._Robot_Wikia

Trump Soho New York hotel and meeting facilities.

https://www.trumphotelcollection.com/soho/manhattan-event-space.php

Untapped Cities, NYC Film Locations for USA Network's "Mr. Robot."

http://untappedcities.com/2015/07/29/10-nyc-film-locations-for-usa-networks-mr-robot/

Wikipedia, several pages.https://en.wikipedia.org/wiki/Main_Page

Episode Three – "Debug"

Episode Number: S01E03

Original Air Date: July 8, 2015

Time: 45 minutes

Synopsis: Elliot strives for a "normal" life but circumstances may thwart him; Wellick attempts to manage his anxiety while waiting for Evil Corp to choose a permanent CTO.

A Slap in the Face

Over a video montage of him working out, Evil Corp's acting Chief Technology Officer, **Tyrell Wellick**, practices the speech he's about to give to the CEO of Evil Corp. He's extremely hard on himself and exacting in his approach and speech patterns. The practiced speech—as painful as it is—ends with him offering up his name as permanent CTO. But before he can even give his speech, the CEO, **Phillip Price**, asks him to come back in two weeks—and mentions that they have already found a "great candidate" for the CTO spot. Afterward, Wellick pays a **homeless man** and pulls on rubber gloves—and then proceeds to beat up the man, leaving him unconscious on the ground as Wellick and his driver,

Mr. Sutherland, drive away.

Notes: The homeless man asks for $300 "this time," implying that Wellick has beaten him up before.

Characters: Phillip Price, the CEO of Evil Corp, is played by **Michael Cristofer**, an accomplished writer and playwright. His play **Shadow Box** won a **Pulitzer Prize**. The homeless man that Wellick beats is played by **Mick O'Rourke**, who also appeared in the Scorsese movie **The Departed**.

Filming Location: According to **Untapped Cities**, the location for Wellick's little "boxing" session is "between Queens Plaza South and 13th Street."

Primary Care Facility

Elliot wakes to find himself in a hospital, recovering from his injuries after being pushed off the railing at Coney Island by Mr. Robot. **Shayla**, his drug dealer, and **Krista**, his psychiatrist, are waiting to speak to him. He'd told the police he'd been jumped by "a bunch of kids" and evidently requested Krista to authorize his discharge. He also apparently refused a full drug panel, and Krista's curious why. "I've been taking morphine," he tells her. She makes him agree to drug testing twice a month, and he's amenable to that—he chose this particular hospital as his primary care facility because the computer system is particularly easy to hack. He'd be able to change the drug test results at will.

Notes: Shayla is Elliot's emergency contact. **William Highsmith** is the head of the IT department—actually, he's the entire IT department for the hospital. He's nearly 70 years old, lives in Queens, and Elliot thinks he's an "idiot—actually, it's not his fault. The people that hired him to secure the hospital's network should have known better." According to Elliot's medical records, he's currently suffering from depression, anxiety, insomnia, mania, lower back pain and "temporomandibular joint dysfunction," a systemic tightening of the jaw muscles better known as TMJ. And his SSN is "672 19 84," which is missing two digits.

Goofs: According to IMDB, in Elliot's drug screen the word "marijuana" is misspelled.

Terminology: Windows 98 is an outdated version of the windows operating system.

Shayla and Darlene

Elliot and Shayla make a purchase at a corner store, then head back to their apartment building. She asks if he had anything to do with "Vera getting busted." Vera is Shayla's supplier and he and his "whole crew" were arrested based on information Elliot sent the NYPD anonymously in **S01E02**. He denies any involvement. They find **Darlene** waiting in Elliot's apartment—she broke in to talk to him. She's surprised at his injuries, but Elliot asks her to leave.

Notes: The sign at the corner market reads "Due to the recent hack on Evil Corp, our credit card systems are not operational. We hope to resolve this matter soon." First, it says "Evil Corp" instead of "E Corp" on the printed sign, so we're clearly seeing the sign through Elliot's "eyes," and he's already "corrected" the name of the company for us. Second, the fact that particular credit cards aren't working shows the far-reaching power of fsociety. According to the tabloids, Jessica Alba wants to join fsociety.

Ollie and Angela

Angela, jogging in the park, returns a dropped wallet to a passerby—but it turns out he was a purse snatcher and the rightful owner yells at Angela for returning it. At home, her boyfriend **Ollie** is on the phone with his other girlfriend, **Stella**—they're just finding out that Ollie's computer has been hacked and that the hackers have nude photos of Stella. Angela returns, and Ollie has to end his phone call quickly.

Angela tells him about the purse snatcher—or tries to, but Ollie cuts her off. He gets another call—it's the **hackers**. They want him to upload a virus to the Allsafe cybersecurity servers, or they'll release "everything" on Ollie and Stella in 100 hours. The hacker, Cisco, hangs up and watches Ollie's panicked reaction through the camera on Ollie's laptop.

Appletinis

Later, at Allsafe, **Gideon Goddard** is holding a meeting in his office. Angela, Ollie and Elliot all work for him—and Gideon's worried. He needs them to double down on their efforts to prevent future hacks of Evil Corp. He also invites them all to dinner at his home that evening, and Elliot passes. Gideon excuses the rest of them and asks about Elliot's injuries. Eliot doesn't want to talk about it—he's created a "cold perfect maze" in his mind to protect himself and his "source code."

Heading back to his desk, Elliot finds Mr. Robot sitting there—he wants to talk. At a nearby bar, Mr. Robot apologizes for pushing him off the railing—and tells him that unless he returns to fsociety, the plan to hack Evil Corp is over. Elliot is overjoyed—he wants nothing more to do with fsociety and returns to work, happier than he's been in weeks. He imagines being normal: drinking Starbucks lattes and asking Shayla to be his girlfriend and attending movies with the normal people. Back at the office, he pokes his head into Gideon's office and surprises him by asking if he still come to dinner tonight—and asks if he can bring his "girlfriend."

Meanwhile, Ollie's decided to go along with the hacker's plans and inserts the infected CD into his work computer. Before he can upload the virus, Angela appears and they leave work together.

Notes: Mr. Robot's preferred drink is the **appletini**. And, at the bar near his work, Elliot pays $12 for his appletini. Elliot thinks the Marvel movies are stupid. According to IMDB, the picture of the dog is a photo from the Instagram page of show creator Sam Esmail's girlfriend, Emmy Rossum. The dog's name is Cinnamon.

Filming Location: According to an article in **InStyle**, the location for the bar where Mr. Robot and Elliot drink Appletinis is the **Racoon Lodge**, located at 59 Warren Street in Tribeca, New York City. The bar closed for good June 30, 2016.

Quotes: Elliot: "This is the world we live in. People relying on each other's mistakes to manipulate one another, use one another, even relate to one another. A warm, messy circle of humanity."

Elliot: "Hey, Gideon. Is that dinner still on for tonight?" **Gideon:** "Um, yeah. Sure. Uh, you want to come?" **Elliot:** "Yeah." **Gideon:** "Great." **Elliot:** "Can I bring my girlfriend?" **Gideon:** "You have a girlfriend?" **Elliot:** "Well, I, uh, haven't asked her yet, but I will. Hopefully she'll say yes." **Gideon:** "Uh, yeah. Sure. Perfect." **Elliot:** "Thanks."

Socializing

Seeing that **Anwar**, a particular male employee of his is at a local club, **Kiss and Fly**, Tyrell Wellick prepares to leave his home. His wife **Joanna** asks if it's necessary, obviously aware of what he's about to do, and Wellick says that everything he does is for their family.

At Shayla's, Elliot asks her to go to the dinner with him as his girlfriend. "I'm not good in social situations like that." She tells her about her interest in sewing and he's impressed, kissing her. She agrees to go with him.

Wellick "happens" to run into Anwar and tells him that he's attracted to Anwar.

At Gideon's, the dinner party gets underway. Gideon's boyfriend Harry makes small talk but Angela seems confused that Elliot has a girlfriend. Gideon thanks Elliot for his good work for Allsafe. Angela and Elliot reminisce about visiting a museum as children.

Elliot gets a news alert on his phone—another data dump of Evil Corp secrets by fsociety. It turns out former CTO Terry Colby had knowledge of the **Washington Township toxic waste** cover-up, a 1993 environmental disaster caused by Evil Corp that killed Elliot's father and Angela's mother, along with 24 other Evil Corp employees. The company beat a class-action lawsuit by the surviving victims, but the latest data dump shows the company was aware their factories were putting out toxic levels of waste and chose to do nothing about it. In a flashback, we see Elliot's mom calling his dad weak for dying and leaving them to fend for themselves.

After Wellick and Anwar have sex at Anwar's apartment, Wellick hacks Anwar's phone.

Notes: The doorbell on Gideon's sweet industrial apartment is broken. Angela and Ollie have been dating for between two and two and a half years—opinions vary. Elliot mentions the "conversation on the plane," which took place in the pilot episode, **S01E01**. Angela and Elliot reminisce about running away at eight years old to the Metropolitan Museum of Art in New York City like **Claudia Kincaid** in "**From the Mixed-up Files of Mrs. Basil E. Frankweiler**" but ended up at the **Queens Museum** instead. When the bus passes by, the scene changes from the flashback to the current day, and Elliot is sitting in the same place on the bus bench as his younger self.

Characters: Joanna Wellick is played by **Stephanie Corneliussen**. Harry, Gideon's boyfriend, is played by **Randy Harrison**.

Goofs: Angela got the idea to run away like Claudia Kincaid from the real-world book "Mixed-up Files of Mrs. Basil E. Frankweiler" but leaves out the "Mrs." when reciting the name of the book.

Hacked

Back at their apartment, Ollie and Angela start to discuss the news about **Evil Corp**, but Angela isn't interested. Ollie tells her about the hack of his laptop, including photos of his other girlfriend Stella ("it meant nothing.") and financial information and nude videos of Angela herself. The **hacker** is demanding that Ollie install a virus onto the Allsafe servers. Angela asks for the CD so she can install the virus herself—she's worried that the hacker has not only her financial information but that of her father, who co-signed her student loan. At Allsafe, Gideon is concerned about some information he's received about the Evil Corp hacks, and reaches out to the **Dulles server farm** for assistance.

Notes: Angela and Elliot bonded over the loss of their respective parents to leukemia from the Evil Corp toxic waste incident. The hacker emails to Ollie are dated around March 27-28, 2015, about four months before this episode aired.

Goofs: When Gideon picks up his phone to call the server farm, it's in **"airplane"** mode and shouldn't be able to make any outgoing calls.

Tied Up

Back at home, Joanna Wellick is waiting up for her husband. She's wearing a mask and there's classical music playing. He sighs and asks if it has to be "tonight" and she says yes. He then proceeds to tie her up and puts a ball gag in her mouth. Back at fsociety, Elliot tells the members that the hack of Evil Corp is back on.

--------------------------------------—

Critique:

This episode gives Elliot a glimpse of what a normal life would be like—dinner parties, quiet discussions with his "girlfriend," and lattes from Starbucks. He seems to take to it temporarily, punctuated by Len's bubbly song "Steal My Sunshine." But the state is only temporary—the pleasant looks on his friends and co-worker's faces can't compete with the revelation that Evil Corp KNEW about how toxic their factories were—an incident that killed Elliot's father—and covered it up. And while it looked like the fsociety plans to hack Evil Corp had been sidelined, by the end of the episode, Elliot had decided to walk away from his new "normal life" and embrace the hack.

Angela's relationship with Ollie is depicted in an interesting way in this episode—while she cares for him, once she finds out about the hack of his laptop and the potential theft of her identity, she becomes almost "robot"-like in her responses. She tell him in a very matter-of-fact voice that they need to break up, then coldly weighs the need to protect her identity with possibly getting her and Ollie fired by going along with the hacker's plans. After a few minutes, she comes back to reality, but there for a moment, she's nearly as robotic—and calculating—as Elliot can be.

Episode Notes:

The episode is titled "Debug:" for most of the episode, Elliot is talking about "bugs" or errors in code—and he thinks he's hidden his "bug" down deep. It's not until the hack of Evil Corp at the end do we discover his bug—his feelings about his father.

References:

NOTE: All sites accessed on August 30, 2016.

IMDB.

http://www.imdb.com/title/tt4730002/?ref_=tt_ep_pr

Mr. Robot Wikia.

http://mrrobot.wikia.com/wiki/Mr._Robot_Wikia

Raccoon Lodge Closing for Good.

http://ny.eater.com/2016/6/30/12068222/raccoon-lodge-dive-bar

Untapped Cities, NYC Film Locations for USA Network's "Mr. Robot."

http://untappedcities.com/2015/07/29/10-nyc-film-locations-for-usa-networks-mr-robot/

Wikipedia, several pages.https://en.wikipedia.org/wiki/Main_Page

Episode Four – "Daemons"

Episode Number: S01E04

Original Air Date: July 15, 2015

Time: 45 minutes

Synopsis: As Elliot is wracked with hallucinations while he attempts to quit morphine cold turkey, the other members of fsociety work to finalize the plan to take down Steel Mountain. Angela has an eye-opening day with Shayla and makes a fateful decision.

Mollify

Lamenting that he's almost out of morphine, **Elliot** explains the hack to the other members of fsociety: they are going to destroy Evil Corp's tape backups, currently being stored in the underground bunkers of a data storage facility called Steel Mountain, by heating up the tapes and destroying the data stored on them. They'll install a special circuit board that gives them remote access to the HVAC systems.

Notes: Elliot describes the Evil Corp tape backups by describing the medium they are stored on: "linear-tape open standard 9, temp value between 61 and 95, iron oxide in mag tape-it sticks to polyurethane with a binder." If they can get the tape backups warmed up to above 95 degrees, the adhesive will "mollify" or become unattached, rendering the tape data unreadable. Steel Mountain's facility is located in a 145-plus acre former limestone mine in the Adirondacks. The facility sports 24/7 armed guards, three-ton steel gates, closed circuit cameras, and NOC (network operations center) staffing.

Terminology: Linear tape is the physical tape backup system used at Steel Mountain. **HVAC** stands for Heating, Ventilation and Air Condition, a standard industrial term for the centralized heating and cooling systems in most buildings. An **asymmetric back door** into a computer system uses a single private key known only to the attacker to access the system. A **Raspberry Pi** is a unique, single-board computer developed by the Raspberry Pi Foundation in the United Kingdom.

Withdrawal

At home, Elliot does the last of his morphine. He's broken his own rules about not abusing the drug—he's out of **Suboxone**, which he used to control his addiction—and now he knows the withdrawal symptoms are coming.

Notes: The path Elliot imagines his morphine took to get to him: biosynthesized in some lab in Mexico, packed into a pill, shipped to the States where it was packaged with a logo and taxed by the government, stolen by a bribed guard, sold to a Vera henchmen, oversold to Shayla and then to him.

Backup

Back at fsociety headquarters, **Romero** has some bad news for the rest of the team—hacking Steel Mountain won't be enough. Evil Corp is physically copying and shipping backups to facilities in Nashville, Colorado, San Jose and Tallahassee. The backups will move on May 1—in just three days—and Elliot decides they need to implement their HVAC plan immediately. Like, they have to leave right now. And **Darlene** will need to coordinate with the Dark Army in China.

Terminology: A **SCADA network** is a "supervisory control and data acquisition" system for remote monitoring and control in industrial situations.

Timeout

Romero and **Mobley** steal a minivan by hacking the alarm and ignition systems, and they head north with Elliot and **Mr. Robot**. But Elliot's withdrawal symptoms kick in, so they crash at a hotel to give him time. Elliot's hallucinating and going through withdrawal while the others wait. Romero complains that this is a waste of time—they should be heading back to NYC to come up with a plan B.

Romero gets frustrated and leaves, and Elliot convinces Mr. Robot that the only logical thing to do is more morphine, enough to get him through the hack. They find a dealer's house and Elliot stumbles inside—but they only have liquid morphine for shooting up.

There is a shooting inside and the girl kissing Elliot is shot twice on the couch right next to him. Then Elliot is shot and falls to the floor, bleeding. On the TV, an fsociety video comes on, then cuts to a scene where Elliot is watching the video being filmed. Mr. Robot gives him a key and another mask. An Evil Corp commercial comes on, followed by Elliot walking down the street where he grew up. First his house is there, and then it's gone, replaced by a sign that reads "Error 404."

Elliot hallucinates Wellick in Elliot's apartment, and then Qwerty, Elliot's fish, starts talking to him. Next he dreams about eating dinner with Angela but they're seated at cubicles like those at their work. Angela is eating a black fish— Qwerty—on a bed of colorful aquarium gravel. He also sees his mother feeding him as a child. Elliot is served raspberry pie and it also contains the key. Angela thinks he's proposing and she says "I do" and the restaurant applauds. Then he's at fsociety in a nice suit and Angela's in a wedding dress and she asks him if he's really going to change the world. She says he's afraid of "his monster" and gives him the key. Next, he's in the room where they film the fsociety videos and puts on the mask. He wakes in the hotel room—it was all a hallucination.

Notes: In the hotel room, Romero and Mobley are watching a scene from the infamous 1995 movie **Hackers** starring Angelina Jolie. And Romero says he bets that somewhere there's a "writer working hard on a TV show that'll mess up this generation's idea of hacker culture." Could he be talking about...**Mr. Robot**, the TV Show? In the dream, Elliot says "hello friend" to the girl on the scooter—this was the title of the pilot episode. The girl and he both sing "Frere Jacques," a nursery rhyme about a man who has "overslept and urged to wake up."

Characters: Qwerty the fish is voiced by **Keith David**, who also appeared in the film **Requiem for a Dream**. According to IMDB, the 2000 film revolves around the "drug-induced utopias of four Coney Island people are shattered when their addictions run deep."

Quotes: Qwerty (the fish): "When you live in a fishbowl, ain't no such thing as change. My entire life's been spent in this thing, my whole world's on your side table. I look around. Same shit, different day. The lighting, the furniture, even the sounds. Always the same. I'm on a loop. And it won't stop unless my life does. I'm exhausted with this world."

Elliot: "Daemons. They don't stop working. They are always active. They seduce. They manipulate. They own us. And even though you're with me, even though i created you, it makes no difference. We all must deal with them alone. The best we can hope for...the only silver lining in all of this...is that when we break through, we find a few familiar faces waiting on the other side."

Army

Back at fsociety, Trenton and Darlene head out to see her **Dark Army** contact. They wait and he finally makes contact—there's a big limo waiting for them. Inside, two men in masks make the women turn over their phones, then drive them to her contact—it's Cisco, the guy that's blackmailing Ollie and Angela. He's also the guy Darlene was dating and broke up with after he proposed to her. He agrees to talk to the Dark Army and move up the timetable.

Filming Location: According to **Untapped Cities**, the Dark Army scenes were filmed at the **Brooklyn Night Bazaar**, a former performance space, game room and market that recently closed.

Walk

Angela gets the hack CD from Ollie's briefcase and visits Elliot, but he's not around. Shayla tells her he's out and invites Angela to walk with the dog with her. Shayla gives Angela some of her Ecstasy. Later, they are in the bathroom at a club and a stoned Angela realizes she's missed several calls from Ollie—and that she has to be at work in four hours. They talk about Angela's propensity for worrying too much—and then they kiss.

Quotes: Angela: "You're not worried?" **Shayla:** "Worried about what?" **Angela:** "I don't know. I always get worried before starting a new job." **Shayla:** "No. I am definitely not worried. Worry's a waste of time. I mean, shit didn't work out at one job, so I got another. That's all! You worry a lot, don't you?" **Angela:** "Yeah."

Gone

Angela arrives at work and uses Ollie's key card to get in. She goes to his computer and uses it to upload the virus, barely avoiding another AllSafe employee arriving early.

Elliot speaks directly to the audience, saying he missed us. He asks "did you leave, or did I?" The members of fsociety climb into their stolen van and get back on the road, heading to Steel Mountain.

Notes: In the final of the episode, the road and mountain in the background form a triangle with a white line going up the middle. This is a callback to the first scene of the episode, where Elliot's last line of morphine is shown on his glass table, stretching out in an identical triangle shape.

--------------------------------------—

Critique:

This episode is insanity, bottled and captured and put on display. The illusions Elliot suffers through as part of his withdrawal illuminate aspects of his personality, but the through-line of the dreams is Mr. Robot and a key that keeps appearing and reappearing. The fever dreams are frenetic in nature and drop hints about other aspect of Elliot's life that we haven't seen yet, including his boyhood home and the street where he grew up. And, interestingly, he's imagining getting married to Angela, but Shayla's the one in this episode actually kissing Angela. Better step up, Elliot, if you're ever going to make that dream a reality.

I enjoyed Shayla and Angela's day out—it felt like a nice, tension-free aside from the main story. I'd love to see a whole episode with these two, just wandering around, walking the dog and talking about Elliot. Maybe they could run into Darlene and all go out and get their nails done together at some nail place.

When he wakes to find himself alone in the hotel room, Elliot experiences real fear—until Mr. Robot appears and reassures him that everything is fine.

Episode Notes:

The title comes from the word "daemon," an old world spelling of the word "demon."

References:

NOTE: All sites accessed on August 31, 2016.

IMDB.

http://www.imdb.com/title/tt4686038/?ref_=tt_ep_pr

Mr. Robot Wikia.

http://mrrobot.wikia.com/wiki/Mr._Robot_Wikia

Untapped Cities, NYC Film Locations for USA Network's "Mr. Robot."

http://untappedcities.com/2015/07/29/10-nyc-film-locations-for-usa-networks-mr-robot/

Wikipedia, several pages.https://en.wikipedia.org/wiki/Main_Page

Episode Five – "Exploits"

Episode Number: S01E05

Original Air Date: July 22, 2015

Time: 44 minutes

Synopsis: Fsociety works to infiltrate Steel Mountain, the location of Evil Corp's tape backups. Vera waits in jail for his release, Angela changes her living situation, and Shayla gets a job.

Spilled Milk

Fernando Vera, now awaiting trial, learns from his lawyer that someone provided the NYPD with an **anonymous tip** and massive amounts of electronic information on Vera's gang and their alleged criminal activities—every tweet or social media post. His younger brother Isaac didn't think their "code" could be broken, but the lawyer says the code was simple. Later, Vera figures it out—Elliot hacked his gang and exposed it to the authorities.

Notes: Vera's lawyer references **The Imitation Game**, a 2014 film about Alan Turing and code breaking during World War II.

Characters: Issac Vera, Fernando's brother, is

played by **Rick Gonzalez**.

Coffee

Elliot and the other members of fsociety wait in a coffee shop as Mr. Robot bumps into a guard who works at the Steel Mountain facility, using an electronic device to **replicate the man's access card** information. They drive onto the grounds, searching for employees they can use as "exploits" to gain entrance to the building. They choose to target **Bill Harper**, a level one sales associate who provides facility tours.

Posing as invented tech billionaire "**Mr. Sam Sepiol**," Elliot follows Harper on a tour of the massive facility, then asks to speak to his supervisor Wendy, who can get him into Level 2, the area of the facility where he needs to plant the circuit board that will allow fsociety to hack the environmental controls and destroy Evil Corp's tape backups. But Wendy doesn't show—it's **Trudy**, another manager. Mobley sends her a fake text and Elliot, trying to access Level 2, runs into **Tyler Wellick**, the Evil Corp acting CTO.

Notes: Steel Mountain's tag line is **"Impenetrable."** Elliot refers to the Steel Mountain employees as potential "exploits," the name of the episode. Steel Mountain has it's own fire department.

Characters: The fictional character's name "Sam

Sepiol" may be an amalgamation of the first name of show creator **Sam Esmail** and the last name of USA Networks development chief **Alex Sepiol**. According to the in-show Wikipedia page for Sam Sepiol, he's an "American computer programmer and businessman widely known as the co-founder of tech start-up company Bleetz," which went public in 2014, earning "Sam" $17 billion after the IPO. During the Steel Mountain tour, Elliot has a flashback of his mother calling him "worthless." Bill Harper, the tour guide at Steel Mountain, is played by **Tom Riis Farrell**.

Filming Location: The "Old Forge Beans" coffee shop is a fictional location created for the show. The exterior shots of "Steel Mountain" were filmed at the **800 Westchester Avenue** complex in Rye Brook, New York. According to **Wikipedia**, the massive complex was built to serve as the headquarters for General Foods.

Wings

Angela is packing—she's leaving **Ollie**, who's begging her to stay. She tells him she uploaded the virus using his PC and ID. At Wings Extravaganza, **Shayla** is training for her new waitress job, then calls Elliot to chat. Later, Angela visits her father and asks to stay at his house for a while. Settling into her room, she finds boxes and bags of past due bills.

Notes: Shayla says she used to be in "pharmaceutical

sales," but the job ended due to "Obamacare."

Characters: Angela's father Don is played by **Don Sparks**, an actor and published songwriter.

Terminology: "Marrying ketchup" involves balancing two bottles on top of each other, the open ends facing each other. Ketchup moves from the top bottle to the bottom, filling it. Be careful when you take the top one off if the bottom one is filled—it can make a mess!

Salad

Wellick is chatting with the financiers of Hezbollah and ISIS while Elliot waits—he's watching a promotional video about Steel Mountain—and joins Wellick for lunch in the cafeteria. Mr. Robot tells him to exploit Wellick's pride and hubris, and Elliot asks if Wellick really eats in a company cafeteria, prompting Wellick to take him downstairs to an executive lounge—on Level 2. Elliot sneaks off and plants the Raspberry Pi device in a utility room light switch. Wellick comes into the bathroom and tells Elliot that he knows Elliot framed Terry Colby, probably because Evil Corp was responsible for the death of Elliot's father. Wellick thinks he's got Elliot all figured out.

Quotes: Tyrell: "I know you framed Terry Colby." **Elliot:** "I didn't." **Tyrell:** "Your father worked at Evil Corp before he died. That's a matter of public record. I'm not turning you in, if that's what you're thinking. I don't even have proof, and even if I did, I don't care. Just wanted to know your weakness. Now I do. Revenge. How ordinary. Just like our waiter. But even extraordinary people, and I believe you are, are driven by human banalities. And unfortunately, we're all human. Except me, of course."

Wine

Tyrell Wellick and his wife Joanna have dinner with Scott and Sharon Knowles. Wellick has heard Knowles might get the CTO job and wants to find some kind of leverage on him. Joanna feigns interest in Scott's wine collection while Tyrell hits on Sharon while she's on the toilet—and she subtly returns his interest.

Characters: Scott Knowles is played by **Brian Stokes Mitchell**, and Sharon Knowles is played by **Michele Hicks**.

Quotes: Tyrell: "So they tapped you for CTO, yes? Don't be surprised." **Scott:** "Suspicious is more accurate. I was beginning to wonder why you set this dinner. Four people in the world know about my conversations. Somehow you're number five." **Tyrell:** "Then I'm exactly what you need in a right hand." **Scott:** "So that's what this is about." **Tyrell:** "Isn't everything about something?"

Toast

The fsociety members return to **Coney Island** in a good mood—the Steel Mountain hack actually worked—but get bad news from Darlene: the Dark Army has backed out of their part of the hack. Darlene wants to start the hack anyway, but Elliot stops her. Back at his apartment, he finds the Shayla's door open and a strange phone on the floor. It rings: the caller is Vera. He knows Elliot turned him and his crew in to the police.

Quotes: Elliot: "My father picked me up from school one day and we played hooky and went to the beach. It was too cold to go in the water so we sat on a blanket and ate pizza. When I got home my sneakers were full of sand and I dumped it on my bedroom floor. I didn't know the difference, I was six. My mother screamed at me for the mess but he wasn't mad. He said that billions of years ago the world 's shifting and ocean moving brought that sand to that spot on the beach and then I took it away. Every day he said we change the world. Which is a nice thought until I think about how many days and lifetimes I would need to bring a shoe full of sand home until there is no beach. Until it made a difference to anyone. Every day we change the world. But to change the world in a way that means anything that take more time that most people have. it never happens all at once. Its slow. Its methodical. Its exhausting. We don't all have the stomach for it."

\-—

Critique:

After last week's hallucination episode, this one felt more like a spy movie or something from the **Ocean's Eleven** universe, as fsociety hacked and cracked their way into the physical Steel Mountain facility. I love how Mr. Robot was literally speaking in Elliot's head through the ear piece. Pretending to be an awkward tech billionaire came easily for Elliot—probably because he's painfully awkward anyway—and watching him break down the tour guide was somehow amazing and awful at the same time.

Wellick and his wife continue to get creepier and creepier, almost reaching Frank and Claire Underwood levels of dastardliness. Between Tyrell hitting on the wife in the bathroom and Joanna sneaking an entire glass of wine while pregnant, I'm wondering how bad these people's karma is going to turn out to be.

Elsewhere, Vera and his brother turn out to be smarter than we were led to believe—and they've figured out who tipped off the police. This could get very ugly very quickly for Elliot and Shayla, right when he's distracted by the final stages of the fsociety hack. Sadly, Angela, Shayla and Ollie didn't have a lot to do on this episode, but they're laying the ground work for more things to come.

Episode Notes:

Elliot refers to the Steel Mountain employees as potential "exploits," the name of the episode.

References:

NOTE: All sites accessed on August 31, 2016.
IMDB.
http://www.imdb.com/title/tt4686038/?ref_=tt_ep_pr
Mr. Robot Wikia.
http://mrrobot.wikia.com/wiki/Mr._Robot_Wikia
Untapped Cities, NYC Film Locations for USA Network's "Mr. Robot."
http://untappedcities.com/2015/07/29/10-nyc-film-locations-for-usa-networks-mr-robot/
Wikipedia, several pages.https://en.wikipedia.org/wiki/Main_Page

Episode Six – "Brave Traveler"

Episode Number: S01E06
Original Air Date: July 29, 2015
Time: 44 minutes
Synopsis: Elliot has two choices: figure out how to hack a jail and get Fernando Vera out, or risk the lives of Shayla, Darlene and himself.

Fight or Flight

Shayla and **Elliot** meet for lunch—he's saying he wish he could have done things differently when **Issac Vera** grabs Shayla and drags her out of the restaurant. **Fernando** speaks to Elliot from prison—Elliot must undo the situation with Vera and his crew or Shayla will die. Issac and **DJ**, another member of Vera's gang, drive Elliot home and tell him to get to work hacking Fernando out of prison. Elliot doesn't think it can be done, and certainly not on such short notice. But they're not taking "no" for an answer.

Darlene drops a bunch of USB drives in the parking lot of a police station, but the hacking exploit installed on the drives is caught by a malware detector. Darlene meets Elliot as he's walking is dog and isn't sorry her exploit didn't work—

she wasn't given enough time. DJ catches them talking and takes them both back to Elliot's apartment.

Notes: The painting in the opening restaurant scene is by Dominican painter **Gilberto Hernandez Ortega**.

Characters: DJ is played by **Jas Anderson**.

Filming Location: According to **Where is Mr Robot**, the lunch scenes were filmed at **Redstone Rocket Lunchpad**, located at 32-35 48th Avenue in Queens, NY 11101.

Terminology: Guisado is a Spanish or Mexican pork stew. According to Elliot, most prisons still use standard **"industrial control systems,"** not unlike those at Steel Mountain, but much less sophisticated. I couldn't find any on-line code resource called **Rapid Nine**, but it sounds similar to other on-line resources like Github or Bitbucket. A **Script Kittie** is a slang term in hacker culture for an unskilled novice who uses scripts or programs to attack networks.

Dig and Dig

Angela is at AllSafe researching the **Washington Township toxic waste scandal**, going through documents from the case and others released during the Evil Corp hack. She tracks down the original attorney in the case, **Antara Nayar**, and tells her that Emily Moss, one of the victims, was her mother. Nayar isn't interested in reopening the case that nearly ended her career unless Angela can somehow produce an inside witness to the cover up.

Notes: There were originally **26 families** represented in the case.

Characters: Antara Nayar, the attorney in the Washington Township scandal, is played by **Sakina Jaffrey**.

Rack and Ruin

Scott Knowles in interviewing potential CTOs when **Tyrell Wellick** strolls in to the conference room and suggests they take the rest of the day off. Scott isn't interested—his wife told him what happened and he offers to let Tyrell watch him go to the bathroom, if that's what he's into. And he tells him to get used to the idea: Tyrell will never be CTO. At home, Tyrell loses it while **Joanna**, his wife, calmly eats.

Terminology: Vacheron and Patek Phillipe Tourbillon are brands of expensive watches; according to **listings on Chrono24**, an on-line watch market, the Patek's start at around $1.6 million.

Done and Gone

Elliot's not having any luck with the hack when **Angela** shows up at his place. DJ and Isaac tell him to get rid of her. Angela tells Elliot about the lawsuit and he encourages her. Back inside, **Mr. Robot** is waiting on the steps—he tells Elliot to call the cops, but Elliot thinks he can come up with a plan that saves everyone.

Elliot heads to the jail to meet with Vera. The plan is to hack the jail network—Elliot left his phone running a wireless sniffer at the security desk—but Vera has to promise to let Elliot and Shayla go or another data dump will be released, exposing his entire operation.

Using the wi-fi network in a passing police car, Elliot hacks the jail. That evening, all of the cell doors open and Vera walks out of jail—and has DJ shoot Isaac. He lets Elliot go and drives away, telling Elliot that Shayla's been in the car with him the whole time. Elliot opens the trunk: Shayla is dead, her throat slashed.

Notes: This is the first death of a major character on the show.

Filming Location: According to **Untapped Cities**, the scene where Isaac almost executes Elliot was filmed at **Newtown Creek**, an industrial waterfront on the border between Queens and Brooklyn, near the Greenpoint Avenue Bridge. And the prison exterior scenes were filmed outside the **Westchester County Correction Facility**, located at 10 Woods Road in Valhalla, NY.

Quotes: Vera: "Told you you'd get her back, bro. You

just didn't realize she was with you the whole time."

---------------------------------------—

Critique:

Tense and frenetic, this episode was the tightest of any since the pilot, piling more and more tension on until the final tragic scene. Elliot is in way over his head and everything with fsociety has to be put on hold as he deals with the repercussions of putting Fernando Vera and his crew in jail.

Watching Elliot continually roll with the punches and invent new hacks on the fly is fun, but the longer the episode went, the more worried I got for Shayla: they never showed her in danger. At no point did they cut to her in a dingy house, tied to a chair. But there really didn't seem to be much to Vera's crew—I guess all his higher ups were jailed in the bust.

I liked Elliot's move, playing the brothers against each other, but it seemed obvious. I was expecting Vera to kill Isaac or Isaac to kill Vera, who turned out to be equal parts psychotic and philosophical. But how did he get word to DJ and arrange for a car to pick them up? It seems like Fernando had the whole plan worked out ahead of time.

Episode Notes:

Fernando's name means "Brave Traveler."

References:

NOTE: All sites accessed on August 31, 2016.

IMDB.

http://www.imdb.com/title/tt4686038/?ref_=tt_ep_pr

Mr. Robot Wikia.

http://mrrobot.wikia.com/wiki/Mr._Robot_Wikia

Patek Philippe Tourbillion.

http://www.chrono24.com/en/search/index.htm?dosearch=true&query=Patek+Philippe+Tourbillon&searchexplain=1&showpage=2&sortorder=1

Untapped Cities, NYC Film Locations for USA Network's "Mr. Robot."

http://untappedcities.com/2015/07/29/10-nyc-film-locations-for-usa-networks-mr-robot/

Where is Mr. Robot, several pages.

http://whereismrrobot.blogspot.com/search/label/S01E06

Wikipedia, several pages.https://en.wikipedia.org/wiki/Main_Page

Episode Seven – "View Source"

Episode Number: S01E07

Original Air Date: August 5, 2015

Time: 48 minutes

Synopsis: A month later, Elliot's still dealing with Shayla's death. Angela's found a way to get Terry Colby to testify, while at Evil Corp, the new CTO is installed and Tyrell Wellick loses control.

Moving Van

The episode begins with a flashback to the day **Shayla** moved in to Elliot's apartment building. **Elliot** awkwardly meets her when she barges into his apartment, hints that she's a dealer, and leaves her fish at his place. She tells him he loves concerts and live music and he tells her he doesn't usually like people, telling her "I wish we already knew each other."

Actually, Elliot's at his psychiatrist's office, staring at a dirty power socket. **Krista** has some forms to fill out—she's releasing him from court-mandated treatment—but she still thinks they have work to do. He returns later for his regular appointment and tells her the truth: he's hacked her and everyone else around her, finding her as lonely as himself.

Notes: Shayla has a regular dealer but might be willing to ask another one, reputed to be a "psychopath," if he can get her **Suboxone** for Elliot—so, it turns out Elliot's the reason Shayla went to Vera—and wound up dead. "Keep the fish, you filthy animal" is an altered version of a quote from the film **Home Alone**—actually, it's a quote from the fake movie shown in Home Alone, "Angels with Filthy Souls," when a character says "keep the change, you filthy animal." And outside in the hallway at Krista's office, you can see the "two paintings" Elliot mentioned in **S01E02**.

Quotes: Elliot: "Sorry I haven't talked to you in a while. I mean, it's only been a month, which I guess in the grand scheme of things isn't that long. Isn't our life like a blip in the cosmic calendar or something? So that's Shayla. A blip. Not even. Here one blip, gone the next."

Duty Bound

Angela and **Antara Nayar**, the attorney on the toxic waste case meet with Tyler Colby's attorneys, seeking his help. They want him to flip on Evil Corp and detail the cover up. **Colby** agrees to meet with Angela, but isn't very cooperative at first. Angela stands up to him and he tells her about the meetings where they decided to cover up the problems, thereby exposing their employees to toxic waste.

Angela tell **Gideon Goddard** that she's going to testify that she broke **chain of custody** on the dat file. She knows it will cost her her job at AllSafe, but it's the right thing to do. Gideon's not so sure—if she testifies, AllSafe will go out of business and everyone who works there will lose their jobs.

Your Honest Self

Elliot's boss at AllSafe, Gideon Goddard, calls him into his office. It's been four weeks since Shayla's death and Gideon tells Elliot he can have more time off if he wants. He warns Elliot about letting Shayla's death close him off from the world again.

But Elliot's thinking about "**view source**," a command in a web browser that lets you read and copy a website's HTML code. With a few changes, the site is yours. He imagines if you could "view source" on people and sees his co-workers with signs around their necks: "I got a nose job," "I love feet," "I pretend to love my husband."

In his apartment, Elliot copies everything he has on **Shayla Nico** to a DVD before destroying his computer. He puts the DVD in his archives, labeling it "The Cure - Disintegration," her favorite song. He's going to miss her. Later, he takes his dog to the vet—**Flipper** has swallowed one of the microchips Elliot removed from his PC when he was destroying the computer.

Mount an Attack

Darlene and **Mr. Robot** discuss fsociety, which the U.S. Government thinks has been sidelined. Mr. Robot wants to get the Dark Army back involved, but Darlene says it's useless—she's been asking and they're not interested. Mr. Robot wants to talk to **Whiterose**, the leader of the Dark Army. Fsociety missed their chance—Steel Mountain shipped tape backups to at least four other facilities, so the new version of the hack is going to have to be far more complicated to wipe out all of Evil Corp's records in multiple locations.

Mr. Robot threatens **Romero** to get him to come back to fsociety, and Darlene meets with Cisco: he's mad she's been using his credentials and asked for a meeting with Whiterose. Cisco's done with Darlene, but the meet will happen. Darlene meets with **Trenton** on the grass of Brooklyn College and convinces her to rejoin fsociety.

Notes: Mr. Robot mentions **Jeh Johnson**, the Secretary of Homeland Security.

Filming Location: Brooklyn College is located at 2900 Bedford Ave in Brooklyn**.** The building shown in **Boylan Hall**, and Darlene and Trenton sit on the grassy expanse just south of the building. In the scenes showing Darlene, you can see the distinctive golden bell tower on top of the Brooklyn College Library.

Fired

Tyler Wellick is sitting though another boring meeting with **Stan**, **Dwight** and **Jeremy**, three slimy Evil Corp. executives. Dwight is bragging how he was "serviced" by a Google hiring executive on the Googleplex volleyball court. Wellick asks about Dwight's children, then fires the three of them in a fit of anger.

Later, **Phillip Price**, the CEO of Evil Corp, introduces **Scott Knowles** as the new CTO. **Sharon Knowles** is with him. Tyrell and **Joanna Wellick** look on—she's pissed off that he didn't get the job. Sharon leaves the party and Tyrell follows her to the bar and propositions her again, inviting her to the roof. She shows up and Tyrell kisses her, then pushes her down and strangles her to death.

Terminology: The **Googleplex** is the corporate headquarters complex of Google, Inc. and its parent company **Alphabet Inc**, located at 1600 Amphitheater Parkway in Mountain View, California.

-------------------------------------—

Critique:

Things take a darker turn for Tyler Wellick and Elliot this episode, which takes place a month after the last.

Elliot's still dealing with Shayla's death, remembering the day she moved in and realizing that it was because of Elliot that Shayla had to start interacting with Fernando Vera, a decision that would ultimately lead to her death. It's not lost on Elliot that she died because of his need for Suboxone—by trying to be responsible and not get addicted to morphine, he caused her death.

And the fsociety hack is on the skids—they missed their opportunity to take down Evil Corp when the Dark Army refused to help out. Now, Evil Corp has physically copied the backup tapes stored at Steel Mountain and moved copies to four other locations. Despite this, Mr. Robot pulls fsociety back together and manages to arrange for a meeting with the illusive leader of the Dark Army, Whiterose. They'll have to come up with an alternative plan if they want to take down Evil Corp.

Wellick's been passed over for promotion, and he takes it out on three employees by firing them. Later, he manages to get the wife of the new CTO alone on the roof of the building and again loses control, strangling her.

Meanwhile, Angela makes her move and gets Terry Colby to turn on Evil Corp and testify on the toxic waste scandal. But is it worth costing her boss, Gideon, and everyone else at AllSafe their jobs?

Episode Notes:

"View source" is a command in a web browser tool that lets you read and copy a website's HTML code.

References:

NOTE: All sites accessed on September 1, 2016.

IMDB.

http://www.imdb.com/title/tt4686038/?ref_=tt_ep_pr

Mr. Robot Wikia.

http://mrrobot.wikia.com/wiki/Mr._Robot_Wikia

Untapped Cities, NYC Film Locations for USA Network's "Mr. Robot."

http://untappedcities.com/2015/07/29/10-nyc-film-locations-for-usa-networks-mr-robot/

Wikipedia, several pages.https://en.wikipedia.org/wiki/Main_Page

Episode Eight – "Whiterose"

Episode Number: S01E08

Original Air Date: August 12, 2015

Time: 45 minutes

Synopsis: AllSafe is hacked and Elliot's meeting with Whiterose is on. The police want to ask Tyrell questions about the death of Sharon Knowles. But it might all be overshadowed by sudden revelations about Elliot and his close companions.

Ballet Class

Darlene wakes up in the high-rise apartment of a rich banker, Xander Jones, after a night together. They discuss the divide between rich and poor and, after he leaves, she searches his apartment and takes a gun from his safe. At ballet class, she runs into Angela, and they chat about their lives and their mutual worry over Elliot and his "shitty month."

Characters: The ballet instructor is played by **James Brown III**, a Broadway singer, actor and dancer who has starred in such TV productions as **The Wiz Live** and **Peter Pan Live**. Xander Jones is played by **Nick Mills**.

Another Way

Elliot's at his psychiatrist's office—last week, he told Krista that he had hacked her and knew many of her most personal secrets. At home, he copies all of Krista's information to a DVD and puts it in his archive.

He meets **Mr. Robot** on the street—the man has managed to recruit all of fsociety back together. Elliot's cracked the problem with Evil Corp storing their backups at multiple locations—the temperature controls in all the facilities are controlled remotely and can be hacked. Fsociety can raise the temperature in all the locations at once and destroy all the tapes. But there are still the physical backups in China. Darlene warns Elliot to be careful, and Mr. Robot agrees.

Notes: At Krista's office, Elliot spends some time looking at the **two paintings** from the pilot episode again.

Firewall

Tyrell Wellick arrives at work, distracted and angry. **Gideon Goddard** from AllSafe is there to speak with him. Gideon tells him about the chain of custody issue, which will result in the charges being **dropped against Terry Colby**, and says AllSafe has improved Evil Corp's network security. After he leaves, Wellick searches the network and finds evidence regarding fsociety. The police arrive—they're questioning everyone in the building because a body was found on the roof.

At home, Joanna is pleased that Wellick supposed slept with Sharon Knowles—now they can move forward with the blackmail plan and Tyrell will become CEO. She doesn't know that Tyrell killed Sharon.

Later, Wellick meets with **Mr. Robot**—Wellick wants to know what they are planning. "We were meant to be allies," Wellick says. He hints that he knows Mr. Robot's "secret." At home, Wellick tells his wife they've been focused on the "wrong players" before the police show up to question him in the death of Sharon Knowles. Joanna fakes her water breaking so the questioning gets delayed.

Characters: Detective Quattlander is played by **Edward James Hyland**, who has appeared films such as **Bridge of Spies** and **The Happening**. Detective Jones is played by **Mark Lotito**.

Terminology: When a computer is **air-gapped**, it is disconnected and physically separated from other networks and computers, thereby putting "air" between them. A **honeypot** is a fake server set up to draw in hackers and trap them, keeping them away from the real network.

Faraday

Gideon arrives to find the AllSafe network is completely down. Elliot investigates the hack and find that the hackers, whoever they are, aren't really going after anything valuable. It's almost like the entire hack is a distraction. Ollie asks Elliot to deliver some drives to "Blank's Disk Recovery on 36th and 5th."

Elliot looks into Ollie's emails and discovers Angela's involved somehow—the hacker has nude photos of her. Elliot meets with Angela and he's angry—if he'd known about this, he could have helped. But Angela is mad too: "**You're never there anymore**. Something is going on with you, Elliot."

Elliot arrives at **Blank's Disk** and is ushered into the back—they have a Faraday cage. A woman enters—it is **Whiterose** and she tells him he has three minutes. They discuss the hack and she says the Dark Army will go through with it in exactly 50 hours and 23 minutes. Before then, Elliot must remove suspicion from himself—Gideon Goddard is watching him, and has installed a **honeypot** to catch fsociety. That's one reason behind the Dark Army hack of AllSafe—to give Elliot time to fix the problem.

Notes: After meeting with Whiterose, Elliot is panicked by the deadline and tells us, the audience, that he wishes he could be more of an "observer," like us. He asks what we would do and wonders if we have more information than he does (we do) and says that's "not fair."

Characters: The elusive Chinese hacker Whiterose is played by well-known actor **B.D. Wong**, best known for playing Dr. Henry Wu in the **Jurassic Park** films and as Father Ray Makuda on HBO's **Oz**.

Filming Location: Elliot and Angela meet next to the fountain in front of the **Chase Bank,** located at 1251 6th Avenue. And according to **WhereisMr.Robot**, the location for Blank's Disks is outside **Nisha Sportswear Inc.**, located at 13 West 36th Street in New York City.

Terminology: An **ASA firewall** is the proper name of a particular type of firewall made by Cisco (the company, not the hacker). A **Faraday cage** is a particular kind of enclosure or room that's built specifically to block electromagnetic signals from entering or leaving.

Darlene

Back at the office, Elliot makes his move to acquire Gideon's phone—he needs it to kill the honeypot. Elliot had **Darlene** remotely attack the phone, draining the battery. When Gideon leaves to watch an fsociety video being broadcast to the office, Elliot goes into his office and acquires the code he needs.

Gideon realizes Elliot's not watching the video and goes to find him. Gideon's faith in Elliot is faltering. But Elliot knows he's a good man—he hacked Gideon long ago—and sends an email as Gideon to shut down the honeypot.

Later, he tells Darlene the plan is coming along. She says she loves him and he **tries to kiss her** and she's repelled. "Did you forget again? Tell me who you think I am." She's Darlene—and she's his **sister**.

Suddenly it all comes back to him—Darlene used to ride her scooter in front of their house and sing "**Frere Jacques**," just like the little girl in his hallucinations in **S01E04**. He asks us, the audience, if we're "freaking out" as well and wonders if we were in on it the whole time.

At home, in the mirror, he sees himself as Elliot and Mr. Robot and the man in the fsociety mask from the videos. He decides he has to hack himself and finds virtually nothing on-line. In his DVD archive of past hacks, the first DVD has nothing written on it. Opening the files, he finds hundreds of pictures of Mr. Robot and a young Elliot. Someone bangs on the door—it's Mr. Robot. He says they should talk.

Notes: Elliot uses Thomson Reuters on-line research tool **CLEAR** to hack himself. Designed for investigators, CLEAR provides comprehensive background checks and information on individuals, including addresses, known aliases, work history and affiliations and more. **According to the website**, CLEAR makes it "easier to locate people, assets, businesses, affiliations, and other critical facts. With its vast collection of public and proprietary records, investigators are able to dive deep into their research and uncover hard to find data."

According to CLEAR, Elliot is 28 and was born on 9/17/1986. His address is not shown—just a P.O. Box, and his SSN is obscured, but it ends in 7250. One of the photos of Elliot and Mr. Robot shows them dressed up as characters from **Back to the Future**: Mr. Robot is Doc Brown, with crazy white hair and a lab coat; Elliot is Marty Mcfly, with a denim jacket and red vest.

Filming Location: The scenes with Elliot and Darlene were shot on Coney Island with the **Wonder Wheel** in the background. Elliot and Mr. Robot had an important discussion on the Wonder Wheel in **S01E01**.

Quotes: Darlene: "Oh my God Elliot! What the f*ck?!" **Elliot:** "I'm ... I'm sorry." **Darlene:** "What the hell is wrong with you?!" **Elliot:** "I'm sorry, I'm sorry, I thought, I just, I'm sorry." **Darlene:** "Oh my God Elliot ... did you forget again? Did you forget who I am?" **Elliot:** "What do you mean? Forget what?" **Darlene:** "Elliot I need you to tell me who you think I am." **Elliot:** "What are you talking about?" **Darlene:** "Tell me right now." **Elliot:** "What are you saying?" **Darlene:** "Elliot?" **Elliot:** "Of course I didn't forget ... you're Darlene. You're Darlene." **Darlene:** "Elliot." **Elliot:** "You're Darlene." **Darlene:** "I'm your..." **Elliot:** "Sister.

You're my sister."

---------------------------------------—

Critique:

Things at AllSafe come to a head when the Dark Army hack begins, but we learn quickly that the whole scheme—the fake CDs from Cisco, the hack of Ollie's laptop, the threat to leak nudes of Stella and Angela—all leads up to ensuring Elliot can meet with **Whiterose**, the head of the Dark Army. It's an interesting conversation in the Faraday cage—whereas Elliot's obsessed with people, Whiterose is obsessed with time. But the result of the very short meeting is the same— the hack is back on, even it means exposing Elliot's secrets.

We see the repercussions of Tyrell Wellick's loss of control last episode—the cops are sniffing around to figure out who killed Sharon Knowles and left her body on the roof of Evil Corp's building. Wellick is not good at controlling his emotional level and starts to get that "horse in a burning barn" look on his face. I think he SERIOUSLY needs to find a homeless man to beat up.

Elliot is happy the hack is going to happen and tells Darlene and then leans in to kiss her. Darlene recoils from Elliot's kiss and wonders if he's "forgotten" who she is again, implying that this has happened before. Her casual intimacy with him has alway seemed strange, but now it all makes sense—she is his sister. And look on her face is similar to that on **Lorraine Baines**—Marty McFly's mother in the **Back to the Future** movies, when she kisses her son **Marty** on the mouth. She doesn't know he's her son—but she says there's something wrong with the kiss. "It's like I'm kissing...my brother," much like Darlene and Elliot. This follows the earlier **Back to the Future** reference when we saw Mr. Robot and Elliot dressed up as characters from the movies.

The show ends by again hinting strongly that Mr. Robot is Elliot's father—the pile of photographic evidence is hard to argue with. What's harder to understand is how Mr. Robot knows to show up at that exact moment so they can talk things out. That's going to be an interesting conversation, I think.

Episode Notes:

The title of the episode comes from **Whiterose**, the elusive leader of the Chinese Dark Army of hackers. And, according to IMDB, whenever they show Elliot's cell phone, the battery is always at 22%

References:

NOTE: All sites accessed on September 1, 2016.

CLEAR by Thomson Reuters.

http://thomsonreuters.com/en/products-services/legal/corporate-and-government-practice/clear.html

IMDB.

http://www.imdb.com/title/tt4686038/?ref_=tt_ep_pr

Mr. Robot Wikia.

http://mrrobot.wikia.com/wiki/Mr._Robot_Wikia

Untapped Cities, NYC Film Locations for USA Network's "Mr. Robot."

http://untappedcities.com/2015/07/29/10-nyc-film-locations-for-usa-networks-mr-robot/

Where is Mr. Robot.

http://whereismrrobot.blogspot.com/search/label/S01E08

Wikipedia, several pages.https://en.wikipedia.org/wiki/Main_Page

Episode Nine – "Mirroring"

Episode Number: S01E09

Original Air Date: August 19, 2015

Time: 49 minutes

Synopsis: Elliot tries to track down some answers about Mr. Robot and Darlene, while Angela and Tyrell Wellick reach turning points in their job prospects.

Pulp Fiction

The episode begins with a flashback to **1994**—we see old computers, CRT monitors, Nintendo consoles and cartridges and old-style tape backup drives. We hear on the radio that the 1994 **World Series** has been canceled, and see **Mr. Robot** sitting at the front desk, working on a floppy disk. The phone rings and he answers it "Mr. Robot;" it's the name of the computer store he runs.

A customer comes in and claims Mr. Robot's son stole money from him. Mr. Robot tells him to leave, then confronts his son **Elliot**. Mr. Robot then offers to take him to see "Timecop" or "Stargate," but Elliot wants to see a different film: "Pulp Fiction."

As they leave to see the movie, we see the exterior of

the "Mr. Robot" shop. Time progresses and we see it change into a dry cleaners, a florist, a tattoo shop and then a branch of Bank of E.

Notes: According to Amazon, because those three films are showing in theaters, that puts this flashback scene somewhere in late October 1994. The "florist" in the Mr. Robot location is named **Washington Township Flowers**, setting this flower shop in the same place where the Washington Township Toxic Waste scandal takes place.

Filming Location: According to WhereisMr.Robot, the exterior shot of the "Mr. Robot" store were filmed at **18 Main Street** in Yonkers, NY. It is currently the home of The Loop Footwear & Clothing.

Goofs: While the "Mr. Robot" location goes through several changes in ownership as time passes, the reflection of the tree branches and leaves—which remain identical throughout—shows that this succession of "shops" was created by the production team over just a few days to simulate the passage of time by showing different shops in the same location.

Important Work

Elliot shouts at Mr. Robot—why didn't he tell Elliot that he was his father and that he was still alive? **Mr. Robot** answers that the work they are doing to bring down Evil Corp.

is more important. Elliot wants answers but Mr. Robot says they need to be careful—and asks Elliot to follow him.

Worried they are being followed, Elliot and Mr. Robot take the **train** to his childhood home in **Washington Township**. They break into their **old family home** and Elliot tours his old room, seeing the window his father pushed him out of. They argue, and Elliot and pushes Mr. Robot out.

Notes: On the train, there are fsociety stickers on the walls and a man is reading a newspaper that shows an article titled "Evil Corp to Release Earnings Report Monday, Substantial Growth Expected" with a photo of Evil Corp CEO Phillip Price. Elliot relates the story of being pushed out his window to Mr. Robot on the Coney Island boardwalk at the end of **S01E02**.

Burnout

Gideon Goddard has a quick breakfast with his boyfriend **Harry**, but he's too nervous to enjoy it. AllSafe has been hacked and Gideon doesn't think the company can recover from the bad press. When he visits **Blank's Disk** to pick up the corrupted hard drives, but there's been a fire. The **entire shop has been destroyed**, along with all of the contents.

Notes: This is the first time we see Gideon's bedroom—the last time they showed Gideon's house was when he invited over several AllSafe employees for dinner in **S01E03**.

Panorama

Angela arrives at **Antara Nayar**'s office—the attorney has been inundated with new information on the Washington Township scandal. Angela wants to work on the case but Nayar says it wouldn't be a good fit. As she's leaving, Angela gets a call from Darlene—she's looking for Elliot and tells Angela that Elliot tried to kiss her last night, forgetting that she is his sister. "You're the one that found him last time he was like this," implying that Elliot has **"forgotten"** important things before.

They meet at the **Queens Museum**, New York Building, and stand over the **Panorama of the City of New York**. Angela is surprised Elliot's not there—"he always came here" when they used to run away together.

Back at her father's house, Angela surfs the Internet and reads stories about Terry Colby, the former CTO of Evil Corp. Her father returns and says he's just seen Darlene in town. Angela goes to Elliot's **childhood home** and finds Darlene—she's still searching for Elliot. They find the remains of the broken window outside. "Hey, wasn't that Elliot's room?"

Notes: The **Panorama of the City of New York**

was built for the **1964 World's Fair** and contained a scaled version of each of the city's 895,000 buildings. Updates were made every few years, and in 1992 the entire model was updated. The model still includes the twin towers of the **World Trade Center**, even though they've been gone for over 14 years in the show universe; to read more about it, **go here**. Angela uses Firefox on her laptop to surf the Internet.

Let Go

In the hospital, **Joanna Wellick** has had her baby. **Tyrell Wellick** looks on with a smile. Joanna tells Tyrell about the other child she had, a girl, when she was fifteen years old. She also tells him to fix the situation with his job at Evil Corp. or she's going to leave him. When he arrives at work, **CEO Phillip Price** is waiting in Tyrell's office. Because the cops are suspicious of Tyrell—Price says he's a "person of interest"—he is being let go.

Characters: The baby in this scene is played by **Declan Dzurkoc** and yes, he has **an IMDB page**.

Mr. Robot

Elliot and Mr. Robot stumble through a **cemetery**. Mr. Robot's hurt and Elliot's helping him along and they end up at a grave. Darlene and Angela are running through the cemetery as well, shouting at him. The grave is Edward Anderson—it's **Elliot's father**. Mr. Robot isn't really there—he's been an **illusion** this whole time. Elliot suddenly realizes he's injured—his head is bleeding and his leg is hurt.

He threw himself out the window.

Darlene and Elliot take the train back into town and she asks him if he remembers when they **started fsociety together**. And Angela returns to her father's home to find Terry Colby waiting—he's got a job offer for her at Evil Corp.

Back at his apartment, Darlene finds his medicine and leaves to refill his prescriptions. Wellick enters a moment later—he knows Elliot is behind everything, including fsociety. He tells Elliot he **killed a woman** only two days ago, strangling her. Elliot takes him to visit the **fsociety headquarters** and Elliot tells Wellick the whole plan, including the plan to destroy the redundant backup files at several Steel Mountain locations.

Notes: Edward Anderson was born 5/9/49 and died 2/28/95. At the train station, Elliot tells Angela: "I'm pretty f*cking far from okay." This is the same line spoken by Marsellus Wallace, a character in **Pulp Fiction**, the movie Elliot and his father went to see at the start of the episode. Wellick takes off his coat and pulls on gloves, just like he did before beating the homeless man in **S01E03**.

Music: When Elliot and Tyrell tour the fsociety

arcade, the song playing is an instrumental version of the Pixies' "Where is My Mind?" by Maxence Cyrin.

Quotes: Tyrell: "How long has this been going on?" **Elliot:** "I don't know." **Tyrell:** "And what is it that you're doing exactly?" **Elliot:** "Encrypting all the files, all the Evil Corp's financial records will be impossible to access. The encryption key will self-delete after the process completes." **Tyrell:** "What about the backups?" **Elliot:** "I took care of that too. China..." **Tyrell:** "Steel Mountain? Of course, even when we went redundant." **Elliot:** "I hacked the AirDream network. I was in all of them." **Tyrell:** "You really thought of everything. Who else was involved?" **Elliot:** " Just me." **Tyrell:** "Well, now it's you and me. I've always told we'd end up working together, Elliot. But still, I have to know. Why did you do it? What did you hope to accomplish by doing all of this?" **Elliot:** "I don't know. I wanted to save the world."

-------------------------------------—

Critique:

Things begin to spin wildly out of control for Elliot as he learns that Darlene is his sister and Mr. Robot, the person who's been following him around—and popping up whenever needed—is his father. They set off on a journey for answers, the answers Elliot has been seeking ever since that ride on the

Wonder Wheel in **S01E01**. Even back then, Mr. Robot would just shake his head and say the answers would have to wait a while.

The trip to his boyhood home is interesting—it reminded me of the similar scenes in the Netflix Marvel series **Jessica Jones**, where she returns to her childhood home.

I was surprised to see that Joanna Wellick had actually had her baby—I saw her walk into the kitchen carrying a glass in the last episode, and between that and the bloody fork thing on the counter (ick), I assumed she'd faked her water breaking. And no pressure, Tyrell, but if you don't get your plan working, you're OUT of the family!

The big reveal paid off nicely, with Darlene and Angela running through the cemetery to keep Elliot from flipping out too much when he finally learned the truth—there was no Mr. Robot. He'd been imagining his father all along—his real father died years ago of leukemia. As a viewer, I wasn't let down, but I remember scenes where people are specifically talking to Mr. Robot and not to Elliot. I guess I'll chalk it up to his delusions, much the same as we, the audience, are seeing through his eyes whenever we see a sign that says "Evil Corp." instead of the real name of the company.

Episode Notes:

Mirroring, the episode title, means to preserve an

exact copy of something in another location to provide better access and security.

References:

NOTE: All sites accessed on September 1, 2016.

Curbed NY, Unlocking the Secrets of New York City's Most Famous Model.
http://ny.curbed.com/2015/2/27/9986444/unlocking-the-secrets-of-new-york-citys-most-famous-model

Declan Dzurkoc IMDB page.
http://www.imdb.com/name/nm7510594/?ref_=nmbio_bio_nm

IMDB.
http://www.imdb.com/title/tt4686038/?ref_=tt_ep_pr

Mr. Robot store location.
http://whereismrrobot.blogspot.com/search/label/S01E09

Mr. Robot Wikia.
http://mrrobot.wikia.com/wiki/Mr._Robot_Wikia

Panorama of the City of New York.
http://www.queensmuseum.org/2013/10/panorama-of-the-city-of-new-york

Untapped Cities, NYC Film Locations for USA Network's "Mr. Robot."
http://untappedcities.com/2015/07/29/10-nyc-film-locations-for-usa-networks-mr-robot/

Wikipedia, several pages.https://en.wikipedia.org/wiki/Main_Page

Episode Ten – "Zero Day"

Episode Number: S01E10

Original Air Date: September 2, 2015 (originally scheduled to air August 26, 2015)

Time: 54 minutes

Synopsis: As the global markets and Evil Corp react to the fsociety hack, Elliot searches for answers from Mr. Robot and former Evil Corp CTO Tyler Wellick. Angela learns more about Evil Corp.

Dog

Krista, Elliot's psychiatrist, meets with Lenny—she knew him as **Michael Hansen**, and they were dating in the first episode. He lied, telling her he was dying to get her to meet with him—he tells her that Elliot hacked him and he's been to the police. Their cyber crime department is looking for him—and they know for certain because Elliot took Hansen's dog **Flipper** to the vet. The dog was microchipped, and a report came back. But his life is in ruins and his wife left him. He wants Krista's help to catch Elliot, but she refuses. Lenny returns to his apartment with takeout food and watches the news—riots are breaking out in Europe over a massive computer hack.

Notes: This is the first time we've seen "Michael Hansen" since the pilot, episode **S01E01**. Krista has a friend at Sloan Kettering. He mentions the real-life **Ashley Madison** hack that happened in July 2015, just a few weeks before this episode aired.

Filming Location: Krista meets him at the same location where they had dinner in **S01E01**, **Pierre Loti**, a real wine and tapas bar located at 300 East 52nd Street in Midtown East. Pierre Loti operates two other locations in New York City.

Terminology: Sloan Kettering is the world's oldest and largest private cancer center, according to **their website**. They were founded in 1884 and are located in New York City

The Hack

Elliot wakes up in an SUV—he doesn't remember where he's been. The parking attendant says it's been **days** and he needs more money, and in cash—the credit card systems are still down. He's confused and asks us, the audience, what we remember, but then adds that he doesn't trust us. Elliot realizes it's Tyrell Wellick's SUV and flees.

Filming Location: The parking lot scene was filmed on the **corner of 17th Street and 6th Avenue in**

Chelsea, beneath street artist Nick Walker's Love Vandal.

Burn Rate

Angela, nervous, arrives at the Evil Corp headquarters. She's late for work—she's been hired to work in the **PR department**. At AllSafe, **Gideon Goddard** is going over his company finances with **Penelope**, his part-time CFO and friend. His burn rate is so high, he'll be out of money soon. She suggests they close the doors—with his primary customer Evil Corp. on the ropes, there's no coming back.

Notes: Gideon mentions "rearranging chairs on the Titanic," a common saying for a hopeless situation. The interviewer mentions the global market reaction and says Evil Corp has lost "more than $400 billion of wealth was lost today."

Characters: Penelope, AllSafe's part-time CFO, is played by **Susan Pourfar**.

Filming Location: Evil Corp is located at the corner of Lexington Avenue and East 57th Street in NYC. The exact address is 135 East 57th Street. According to **Untapped Cities**, this is the same building used as the offices of Norman Osborn in the first **Spider-Man** movie.

Quotes: Penelope: "Gideon, I handle the money. It's always going to be a depressing conversation."

Terminology: A **burn rate** is how fast a company is

losing money after all profits and expenses are calculated. Many tech companies and startups have a high burn rate as they race to become profitable or launch a product or service.

Burned

At fsociety headquarters, they're destroying all the hard drives and computers. Elliot arrives and everyone's mad at him for EXECUTING the hack without them. He's confused. **Darlene** says he disappeared from the apartment—she'd gone out to get his meds—and has been gone for three days.

Elliot doesn't remember and wonders what happened with Wellick. He gets on-line and reads about the **massive hack** to Evil Corp's data center—a "weekend" breach has "reportedly eliminated all record of individual and corporate debt owed to the company." The NSA is searching for fsociety, who take all the computer parts to a dog shelter, where they get access to a burn room normally used to cremate dead animals. On her way out, **Trenton** and the others pick the locks and lets all the dogs free.

Notes: The earlier breach is now known as "the **Colby Scandal**." The news reports, all dated 5/12/15, also mention the hack in China to destroy backups stored at "Evil Corp's Chinese data centers" and "wide-scale" credit card system outages. Popular website **io9** shows a headline that reads "Five Steel Mountain Facilities Could Also Be Involved in Systemic Hack." Io9, a division of **Gawker Media**, reports on tech news among other subjects. A longer article speculates that fsociety formed in late 2014 and mentions the Federal Reserve's potential response.

Panic

Elliot arrives at Evil Corp to find the employees in a panic. Elliot can't figure out why Tyrell Wellick didn't stop the hack—Elliot remembers telling him the whole plan. Elliot goes to Wellick's home but he's not there, but **Joanna** is. He's immediately creeped out by her and asks us, the audience, for our help. "I feel like she can hear us." He tells Joanna his name is "Ollie."

Notes: Elliot says the worm took Darlene maybe two hours to code. As he walks through the Evil Corp offices, they show President Obama on a television, meeting with his "cabinet members" to formulate a response to the global hack.

Quotes: According to IMDB, what Joanna says to Elliot on the street in front of their home means in Danish: "if you did something to him, I am going to kill you." Interestingly, this is also apparently the only foreign language through the whole season that isn't subtitled.

Terminology: A **worm** is a program that makes data unreadable. **256-AES** is an encryption methodology, or

Advanced Encryption Standard, that uses a key that is 256 bits long. According to **an article on encryption levels at EE Times**, it "would take 1 billion billion years to crack the 128-bit AES key using a brute force attack. This is more than the age of the universe (13.75 billion years.)"

End of the World

Back at Wellick's SUV, Elliot calls out for Mr. Robot to appear, but he doesn't show up. Elliot searches the car and finds a **USB drive** hidden in a pair of sunglasses.

At fsociety, Darlene asks the other members of fsociety to hand out party fliers as their last official act together as a group. The others are depressed and wonder what happened to their "fearless leader" Elliot. He's at a cyber cafe and opens the USB drive, which contains a video titled "**Boardwalk Fail**" that shows Elliot sitting on the railing at Coney Island and then jumping off.

Elliot realizes he has to force Mr. Robot's hand and calls the police to confess. **Mr. Robot** appears. Elliot throws him against a wall and strangles him, demanding to know where Wellick is. Mr. Robot reminds him: "you know how weird this looks, right?" and we cut to what everyone else is seeing—Elliot holding HIMSELF by the neck against the wall. Elliot doesn't care. Mr. Robot gets Elliot punched in the face.

The End of the World Party gets underway, and

Darlene chastises the others for not being happier with what they've accomplished.

Notes: The actual skateboarding video show during this episode is available to watch on-line at Vimeo, uploaded by a user named "sk84904." The **link is here**. The party invitation says "End of the World Party." Between those words are written "Or How I Stopped Worrying and Learned to Love Fsociety." This is a play on the film **Dr. Strangelove**, with features a secondary title of "How I Stopped Worrying and Learned to Love the Bomb." The flyer also says the party will feature **DJ Mobley** and offer "free booze." The party will be at the Coney Island Arcade and run "tonight 9pm to ???" The video shows that Elliot was alone at the end of **S01E02** when he's supposedly talking to Mr. Robot and was "pushed" off. When we see Elliot holding himself against the wall, this is the first time we see one of his **Mr. Robot delusions** from someone else's perspective.

Characters: The huge guy that punches Mr. Robot/Elliot in the face for insulting his wife? He's played by **Adrian Matilla** and officially listed in the cast as "Huge Guy."

Evil Corp

At Evil Corp, **James Plouffe** prepares to go on TV for a live interview. He's the Executive Vice President of

Technology, so he probably works for CTO Knowles, and Angela works for him now. She helps him find a bag of missing paperwork he's looking for. On the air, he answers questions and addresses concerns about the hack. Pushed into a corner, he agrees with the interviewer: the public should be worried. He then reaches for his bag, pulls out a gun, and shoots himself on live TV.

Afterward, CEO **Phillip Price** talks to the police and then sits with Angela, who has blood on her shoes. She goes out to shop for new shoes and argues with the clerk, who chastises her for working at Evil Corp. Back at work, she chats with Price, who's impressed with her and is happy that Plouffe killed himself. "He was weak." Price then speaks to the gathered company personnel and **lauds Plouffe** for his bravery. Angela realizes that she's surrounded by evil.

Notes: The on-air suicide of Plouffe has some similarities to the real life on-air suicide of **politician R. Budd Dwyer** on January 22, 1987. The Pennsylvania politician killed himself in front of gathered reporters and others during a news conference. He had been convicted of receiving a bribe and was due to be sentenced the next day.

Filming Location: The interview scene was shot in the **SoHi conference room** at the **Trump Soho**, located at 246 Spring Street in New York City. Checking out the hotel website, you can review their **meetings section and see**

photos of the SoHi conference room—it's at the top of the building on the 46th floor, measures 34 x 56 feet, and features a 13 foot-high ceiling. This is the same room used in the board room scene in **S01E02**, when Wellick offers Elliot a job. And after the suicide, Angela heads to **L.K. Bennett** at 655 Madison Avenue for a new pair of shoes and a lecture. Phillip Price address the gathered employees of Evil Corp at **Gotham Hall**, a former bank and current event space. Built between 1922 and 1924 as the Greenwich Savings Bank, it has become an event space and is available for rent.

Times Square

In Times Square, protesters are marching, cheering on fsociety for the massive hack. Mr. Robot and Elliot are arguing—Elliot wants to know what happened to Wellick. Elliot asks us, the audience to help. "Stop talking to them," Mr. Robot says. "They can't help us." Elliot's mother and a younger version of him appear, saying Mr. Robot is right. Elliot says none of them are real. "Neither is whoever you're talking to," Mr. Robot says, talking about us, the audience.

Surrounded by chanting crowds, Elliot wishes he could be alone. **Everyone disappears**, including Mr. Robot, and Elliot's left alone in a silent Times Square. Mr. Robot appears on one of the advertising screens, telling Elliot he needs to trust him. Elliot complies and walks to the subway, heading home. He watches the news on his computer, enjoying the "**beautiful carnage**" he's created. There is a knock on the door, and he goes to open it—and the screen goes black.

Notes: Mr. Robot, being part of Elliot, knows that we, the audience, exist.

Quotes: Mr. Robot: "Is any of it real? I mean, look at this, look at it! A world built on fantasy! Synthetic emotions in the form of pills! Psychological warfare in the form of advertising! Mind altering chemicals in the form of food! Brainwashing seminars in the form of media! Controlled isolated bubbles in the form of social networks. Real? You want to talk about reality? We haven't lived in anything remotely close to it since the turn of the century! We turned it off, took out the batteries, snacked on a bag of GMOs, while we tossed the remnants into the ever expanding dumpster of the human condition. We live in branded houses, trademarked by corporations, built on bipolar numbers, jumping up and down on digital displays, hypnotizing us into the biggest slumber mankind has ever seen. You'd have to dig pretty deep, kiddo, before you can find anything real. We live in a kingdom of bullshit, that even you have lived in for far too long. So don't tell me about not being real: I'm no less real than the f*cking beef patty in your Big Mac. As far as you are concerned, Elliot, I am very real. We are all together now, whether you like it or not."

The Estate

After the credits start, another scene begins with the exterior of an opulent mansion. Whiterose arrives in a limo, this time dressed as a man, and enters the party, chatting with Evil Corp. CEO Phillip Price. They discuss another business deal, then get to the matter at hand: the hack. Whiterose thinks Price knows who is behind the hack, and Price confirms it, saying they will deal with it.

Notes: In the final scene, the harpist is playing "**Nearer My God to Thee**," a song famously played on the Titanic as the great ship was sinking. There was an earlier allusion to the **Titanic** when Gideon felt like all of his efforts to save AllSafe were nothing more than "rearranging the chairs" on the Titanic.

Filming Location: The mansion shown in the last scene is the famous **Hempstead House**, located at 1217 Middle Neck Road, Sands Point, New York. The mansion, also known as the **Gould-Guggenheim Estate**, was built in 1912—interestingly, the same year as the **Titanic** sunk, a recurring theme of this episode. The estate grounds actually contain two castle-like buildings: the Hempstead House and Castle Gould, a smaller home. The **building's website states** that the location is available for magazine shoots, commercials and other productions.

-------------------------------------—

Critique:

The season finale arrives and delivers us the promise of the entire season—a world in financial chaos. And Elliot's missed the whole thing, spending days in an SUV in a parking lot. Skipping over the details of someone spending 48 hours in a van—did he eat anything?—Elliot realizes the hack has happened and sets out to find out why. Wellick knew the whole plan, so why did he let it happen? And where is he?

Elliot spends the episode searching for Wellick. In the final moments of the last episode, Elliot glanced at the popcorn machine, where Darlene stashed her gun. How did Elliot know the gun was in there? Did he/Mr. Robot kill Wellick to prevent him from stopping the hack? Then what was the point of telling him the whole plan?

Everyone else is dealing with the repercussions of the hack—Evil Corp is scrambling to deal with the destruction of all of their financial records, citizens around the world are rising up, and Angela and Gideon are dealing with changes in their lives. Angela has taken the PR job at Evil Corp. But by the end of the episode, she realizes she's sinking deeper into the soulless corporation. Gideon looks like he's on the ropes as well—his company is burning cash and he seems hopeless.

Elliot struggles to deal with his imagined father, soon to be joined by an imagined mother and younger version of himself. The scenes in Times Square bring home Elliot's deep delusions, including the ominous silence of an empty space that's usually filled with so much bustle and commotion. Elliot is lost and alone even when he's surrounded by others— and in the end, he finally realizes that he's truly alone. Mr. Robot is in charge and Elliot knows it, following his instructions.

It doesn't really matter at this point—there is nothing Elliot or anyone else can do to reverse the hack. This episode is about people dealing with things that have already happened. While everyone else in the world is dealing with the fallout of the hack—there are many scenes of worried world leaders scrambling to react to the computer breach or reassure the public—Elliot's dealing with what he learned in the cemetery last episode. He's alone and he's been alone all along.

There's a nice scene where Mr. Robot walks over and insults a man in the coffee shop, showing that we can't trust Elliot's perception of where "he" is and where "Mr. Robot" is in the world. In his mind, he's still standing against the wall, watching Mr. Robot cross to the man and insult him. But we know—but never see—that it's actually Elliot that crosses to the man and insults him. He's imagining himself watching Mr. Robot get punched. This scene explains some of the past scenes where we've seen Elliot watching Mr. Robot talking to others or when Mr. Robot is alone, talking to people. We understand now that it was Elliot all along.

The show ends with a mystery: who's at the door? There are several options. It could be Wellick, still alive and furious at Elliot for going through with the hack. Or it could be Michael Hansen, who has tracked Elliot down and angry at him for ruining his life. I think it's probably Darlene, still mad at Elliot for missing the "end of the world" party.

Or maybe it's the NSA or the FBI.

The after credits scene reminded me of **Eyes Wide Shut**, with the long tracking shot through opulence that seems completely unthreatened by the chaos outside. We see the 1% drinking champagne served by beautiful women— notice that the only women in the mansion act as servants to a group of very wealthy men—and talking about matters of finance and power. Price doesn't even seem that upset over the hack that threatens to destroy his company. Whiterose, appearing for the first time since **S01E08** and this time dressed as a man, hints that Evil Corp needs to deal with Elliot. And Price says they will soon enough.

Episode Notes:

Although he's mentioned several times, Tyler Wellick is not seen during this episode. **"Zero Day,"** the title of the episode, refers to the day when a computer program is scheduled to attack. According to IMDB, this episode was originally scheduled to air on August 26 but was delayed due to **a shooting that occurred in Roanoke, Virginia earlier in the day**. Two members of a local news team were reporting live in Roanoke when they were approached by a disgruntled former employee of the station and shot. Both were killed, and the gunman was chased in a manhunt that lasted nearly five hours before the shooter shot himself. The network delayed the airing of this episode over concerns about a backlash over a scene—the one of Plouffe killing himself live on the air—in the episode's finale.

References:

NOTE: All sites accessed on September 2, 2016.

AES Encryption.

http://www.eetimes.com/document.asp?doc_id=1279619

Gotham Hall. http://www.gothamhallevents.com/

IMDB.

http://www.imdb.com/title/tt4686038/?ref_=tt_ep_pr

Mr. Robot Wikia.

http://mrrobot.wikia.com/wiki/Mr._Robot_Wikia

Pierre Loti Midtown.

http://midtown.pierrelotiwinebar.com/

Roanoke Shootings on August 26, 2015.

https://en.wikipedia.org/wiki/Murders_of_Alison_Parker_and_Adam_Ward

Skateboarding video on Vimeo.

https://vimeo.com/user43240456

Sloan Kettering Cancer Center.

https://www.mskcc.org/

Trump Soho New York hotel and meeting facilities.

https://www.trumphotelcollection.com/soho/manhattan-event-space.php

Untapped Cities, NYC Film Locations for USA Network's "Mr. Robot."

http://untappedcities.com/2015/07/29/10-nyc-film-locations-for-usa-networks-mr-robot/

Wikipedia, several

pages.https://en.wikipedia.org/wiki/Main_Page

Mr. Robot: A Binge Guide to Season 1

Cover Design by Greg Enslen

Published in the United States of America

For more information, please see the author's website at

www.gregenslen.com.

About the Author

Greg Enslen is an Ohio author and columnist. He's written and published nineteen books, including five fiction titles, several non-fiction guides and four collections of newspaper columns. Several are available through Gypsy Publications of Troy, Ohio. To receive updates on upcoming titles, sneak previews and appearances, subscribe to his mailing list, "**A Murder of Crows**." For more information, please see his **Amazon Author Page** or visit his **Facebook fan page**. Find out more **www.gregenslen.com**.

Books by Greg Enslen

All titles are available on Kindle:

Fiction
Black Bird

The Ghost of Blackwood Lane

The 9/11 Machine

Frank Harper Mysteries
A Field of Red

Black Ice

Guide Series
A Field Guide to Facebook

A Viewer's Guide to Suits for Season 1

A Viewer's Guide to Suits for Season 2

A Viewer's Guide to Suits for Season 3

Game of Thrones: A Binge Guide for Season 1

Game of Thrones: A Binge Guide for Season 2

Game of Thrones: A Binge Guide for Season 3

Game of Thrones: A Binge Guide for Season 4

Game of Thrones: A Binge Guide for Season 5

Mr. Robot: A Binge Guide for Season 1

Newspaper Column Collections

"Tipp Talk" Newspaper Column Collections

for years 2010, 2011, 2012, and 2013

Can I Ask A Favor?

Thank you for reading this book - I hope you enjoyed it. If you enjoyed this book, found it useful or otherwise then I'd really appreciate it if you would post a short review on Amazon. If you could, take a few minutes out to write a review of this book on **Amazon**, **Goodreads**, Facebook or any other place you feel like sharing.

If you'd like to leave a review for one of my books, please visit the link below: **http://bit.ly/geauthor** Reviews are the best way readers discover new books. And, believe it or not, the sheer number of Amazon reviews affects how Amazon lists book titles. So swing over there and jot down a couple of sentences. Good or bad, every review helps increase the "social buzz" of the book. I would truly appreciate it.

— Greg Enslen

Printed in Great Britain
by Amazon